CATHOLIC DELIVERANCE MANUAL

Robert Abel

Valentine Publishing House
Denver, Colorado

Valentine Publishing House LLC
P.O. Box 27422, Denver, Colorado 80227

The Scripture quotations contained herein are from the *New Revised Standard Version Bible: Catholic Edition,* copyright 1993 and 1989 by the Division of Christian Education of the National Council of the Churches of Christ in the U.S.A., and are used by permission. All rights reserved.

Excerpts from the second edition of the *Catechism of the Catholic Church* for the United States of America, copyright © 1994, United States Catholic Conference, Inc.—Libreria Editrice Vaticana. English translation of the *Catechism of the Catholic Church: Modifications from the Editio Typica* copyright © 1997, United States Catholic Conference, Inc.—Libreria Editrice Vaticana.

Cover Graphics by Desert Isle Design LLC.

Publisher's Cataloging-in-Publication Data
    Abel, Robert.
    Catholic Deliverance Manual / Robert Abel

    p. cm.
    ISBN-10 : 0-9994908-0-X
    ISBN-13 : 978-0-9994908-0-8

    1. Deliverance.
    2. Catholic Church.
    3. Spiritual Warfare.

    BX2350.3 .A24 2018
    248.4' 82–dc21

Printed in the United States of America.

"*Catholic Deliverance Manual* is an excellent resource that enables the reader to recognize and safely cope with personal problems effectively. It's truly a god-send, especially when skilled assistance is rare, expensive and hard to find. In this insightful book, Robert Abel provides the reader with effective forms of protection against the most common types of demonic attack. By overcoming *temptations, infestations, depressions, obsessions, oppressions, possessions* and *subjugations,* this book fulfills all the informational needs for embattled souls, while providing enlightenment for every reader."

FATHER JOHN H. HAMPSCH C.M.F.

Put on the whole armor of God, so that you may be able to stand against the wiles of the devil. For our struggle is not against enemies of blood and flesh, but against the rulers, against the authorities, against the cosmic powers of this present darkness, against the spiritual forces of evil in the heavenly places.

Ephesians 6:11–12

TABLE OF CONTENTS

An Introduction to the Enemy.................................1

The Mechanics of Spiritual Warfare 9

Communicating with Demonic Spirits........................19

Denouncing the Sin of Divination............................33

Talismans, Amulets & Good Luck Charms.................39

Alcohol, Marijuana & Pharmaceutical Drugs..............47

Breaking Sinful Agreements with Evil........................59

Sexual Immorality & Unhealthy Soul-Ties 69

Avoiding Unhealthy Relationships 81

Taking Negative Thoughts Captive 91

The Redemptive Value of Suffering............................99

Dream Channeling with Fallen Angels 111

Receiving Demonic Impartations 119

Vows & Spiritually Binding Agreements....................131

The Sin of Idolatry Occurs in the Heart...................145

Beware of Demonic Religious Spirits.........................153

Interaction with Fallen Angels of Light 161

Praying to Unknown Spiritual Entities 169

The Importance of Emotional Healing 181

Renouncing Lodges & Secret Societies 197

Denouncing Cults that Deny the Trinity.................203

Developing a Deeper Relationship with God...........215

Notes 224

AN INTRODUCTION TO THE ENEMY

In the beginning, before God created the heavens and the earth, everything existed in perfect harmony. God's loving kindness and mighty power were displayed in glorious splendor upon a magnificent throne that was surrounded by angelic beings who worshiped him day and night.

Then one day everything changed. When God disclosed his plan to create Adam and Eve from the dust of the ground for the purpose of establishing loving relationships with their offspring, it made one of the highest-ranking angels very jealous. It was Lucifer's job to receive orders directly from God and forward those assignments to the lower-ranking angels. When God gave a command for one of the cherubim to follow, Lucifer would add a little extra information in an attempt to transmit a slightly different meaning.

If one of the lower-ranking angels questioned the logic of the command, Lucifer would add even more confusion in an attempt to cast a shadow of doubt upon God's intentions. After Lucifer had sown seeds of doubt in a third of the heavenly host, he gathered his followers together to present his case. As soon as Lucifer disrupted the harmony that flowed so smoothly from the heavenly court, a war broke out in heaven. According to the Book of Revelation, *Michael and his angels fought against the dragon. The dragon and his angels fought back, but they were defeated, and there was no longer any place for them in heaven.*

The great dragon was thrown down, that ancient serpent, who is called the Devil and Satan, the deceiver of the whole world—he was thrown down to the earth, and his angels were thrown down with him. Rejoice then, you heavens and those who dwell in them! But woe to the earth and the sea, for the devil has come down to you with great wrath, because he knows that his time is short![1]

After Lucifer and a third of the heavenly host were cast out of heaven, God stripped them of their angelic powers and took away their spiritual gifts. Everything that made these angels beautiful was stripped away. The only thing that remained was complete darkness, hate and a vengeful desire to destroy humanity.

Although Lucifer tried to reestablish the same hierarchical order that existed in the heavenly court, it was impossible. The highest-ranking angels that ruled over the thrones and dominions were constantly fighting with the lower-ranking angels that governed the principalities. The fighting continued in the outer abyss until the day Satan called for a truce by saying, "Stop fighting among yourselves! Let's get even with God by attacking his beloved creation."

"How is that possible?" one of the generals asked.

"If we can trick Adam and Eve into disobeying one of God's laws, then that sin will separate those despicable little creatures from God's blessings and protection. Once Adam and Eve become separated from God's fellowship, we can attack them even more, driving them into complete darkness."

"That's a great idea!" the general said.

Because Satan is a highly intelligent spiritual being, he was able to disguise his true identity in the form of a serpent. After slithering in the shadows through the covering of the tall grass, he waited for the perfect opportunity to strike. When Eve was alone in the garden, the serpent said to her, *"Did God say, 'You shall not eat from any tree in the garden'?"*[2]

Startled by the voice, Eve turned around and said, *"We may eat of the fruit of the trees in the garden; but God said, 'You shall not eat of the fruit of the tree that is in the middle of the garden, nor shall you touch it, or you shall die.'"*[3]

The serpent slowly coiled his camouflaged body into a circle, raised his head off the ground and said, *"You will not die; for God knows that when you eat of it your eyes will be opened, and you will be like God, knowing good and evil."*[4]

After thinking about what it would be like to obtain spiritual powers, Eve approached the tree in the center of the garden. She noticed that the *tree was good for food, and that it was a delight to the eyes.*[5] Because Eve wanted to acquire supernatural powers and become wise, she *took of its fruit and ate; and she also gave some to her husband, who was with her, and he ate.*[6]

After disobeying God's command and committing the first sin, Adam and Eve noticed a shift in the spirit realm. Their eyes were opened, *and they knew that they were naked; and they sewed fig leaves together and made loincloths for themselves.*[7] Later that evening when Adam and Eve heard the sound of the Lord walking in the garden at the time of the evening breeze, they *hid themselves from the presence of the Lord God among the trees of the garden. But the Lord God called to the man, and said to him, "Where are you?"*[8]

Adam responded by saying, *"I heard the sound of you in the garden, and I was afraid, because I was naked; and I hid myself."*[9]

Then God said, *"Who told you that you were naked? Have you eaten from the tree of which I commanded you not to eat?"*[10]

Adam responded by saying, *"The woman whom you gave to be with me, she gave me fruit from the tree, and I ate."*

Then the Lord God said to the woman, "What is this that you have done?"

The woman said, "The serpent tricked me, and I ate."[11]

All the devil needed to do was distort a few facts and raise a few questions about God's intentions, and he caused Adam and Eve to commit the first sin. After the first sin had been committed, the destructive consequences of Adam and Eve's actions were then passed on to the rest of humanity in the form of original sin. God being pure love, light and truth could no longer interact with his beloved children the same as before.

After Adam and Eve had fallen from grace, the Lord said, *"See, the man has become like one of us, knowing good and evil; and now, he might reach out his hand and take also from the tree of life, and eat, and live forever." Therefore the Lord God sent him forth from the garden of Eden, to till the ground from which he was taken. He drove out the man; and at the east of the garden of Eden he placed the cherubim, and a sword flaming and turning to guard the way to the tree of life.*[12]

After Adam and Eve had been driven out of paradise, Satan unleashed his army of fallen angels. The first deadly assault occurred when demonic spirits filled Cain's heart full of rage and incited him to kill his brother. It didn't take very long before the entire world was filled with darkness. After several generations had passed, the *Lord saw that the wickedness of humankind was great in the earth, and that every inclination of the thoughts of their hearts was only evil continually. And the Lord was sorry that he had made humankind on the earth, and it grieved him to his heart.*[13]

Although it broke God's heart to watch Lucifer and his vast army of fallen angels tempt humans into committing sin and harming each other, he allowed the deadly assaults to continue for the purpose of our own spiritual growth. Although it was originally God's intention to create a tropical paradise where humanity could live in perfect harmony, he moved the time frame for humanity's entrance into paradise further into the future, and decided to use this world as a testing ground.

The perfect state of paradise that every man and woman desires still exists and is waiting for us in heaven, but before we can enter our heavenly home, we must first pass the test of life. Because Satan and his vast army of fallen angels have been given permission to tempt humanity, the purpose of this life is *not* to have fun, or to pursue happiness through material possessions; the purpose of this life is to prove our loyalty to God.

God allows the devil and his vast army of fallen angels to tempt humans because he wants to see who will be faithful to his commandments and who will disobey his laws and betray his love. God wants to test everybody's hearts for the purpose of determining our status in his eternal kingdom. He wants to know if we will serve him in obedience, or if we will allow ourselves to be seduced by the devil. The only way for God to know where our loyalties reside is to test us with real-life situations. If we pass the test, we can enter paradise for all eternity. If we fail the test, we will receive the same condemnation as the devil and his fallen angels.

Because the devil has the right to remain in this world for the purpose of tempting anyone he wants, there is *not* any kind of magic charm that a person can use to make the devil go away. In the event that you find yourself being harassed by fallen angels, you can command them out of your life in the name, power and authority of Jesus. In the event that the demonic attacks continue, it usually means you have entered into a sinful agreement with evil, and that agreement is giving demonic spirits the right to remain in your life.

The only way to completely drive evil out of your life is to denounce all sinful agreements and continue growing in holiness and obedience to the Lord. Because Satan and his vast army of fallen angels are highly intelligent spiritual beings, they will do everything within their power to disguise their sinful agreements in the form of a blessing. That way, a person will think he or she is receiving a benefit from the spirit realm, and instead of viewing the sinful agreement as the source of the attack, that person will tend to cherish it as a gift.

A good example of the way the devil disguises his sinful agreements in the form of a blessing comes from the fall of Adam and Eve in the Garden of Eden.

Because Satan was able to present the temptation as a spiritual benefit, Eve considered the devil's offer and *saw that the tree was good for food, and that it was a delight to the eyes, and that the tree was to be desired to make one wise.*[14]

In the same way that Satan was able to disguise Adam and Eve's temptation in the form of a blessing, he continues to use the same tactics of deception today. If the devil offered Eve a piece of fruit and said, "By eating this fruit, you will be giving me access to your life, and once I gain access to your life, I will destroy your relationship with God," then Eve would have refused the devil's offer. Because the devil always presents his temptations in the form of a seductive benefit, it makes them very difficult to identify and even harder to resist.

In an effort to remain hidden and undetected, the devil will *not* attack a person immediately after he or she enters into a sinful agreement; instead, the demonic spirits will make that person feel spiritually blessed. The deceptive spirits will use the same tactics to draw that person back for more sin, and once a person feels comfortable with his or her sinful agreements, the devil will start the assault. That way, the person will never suspect the sinful agreement as the source of his or her problems.

By studying the examples in the following chapters, you will be able to see how demonic spirits use cleverly crafted sinful agreements disguised in the form of blessings. After you break all agreements with evil, you will be able to drive the devil out of your life and sphere of influence in the name, power and authority of Jesus.

THE MECHANICS
OF SPIRITUAL WARFARE

Because there's a lot of confusion surrounding the topic of spiritual warfare, it may be helpful to clarify a few basic terms that will be used throughout this book. The first subject that needs to be addressed is who has authority to drive evil spirits out of a person's life. The answer to that question is only God has authority over demonic spirits. Satan and his vast army of fallen angels are highly intelligent spiritual beings, and even though they have been stripped of their powers, they still make a formidable adversary.

A good example of the power that demonic spirits possess comes from a group of Jewish exorcists who watched the Apostle Paul casting out demons in the name of Jesus. According to the Acts of the Apostles, *God did extraordinary miracles through Paul, so that when the handkerchiefs or aprons that had touched his skin were brought to the sick, their diseases left them, and the evil spirits came out of them.*

Then some itinerant Jewish exorcists tried to use the name of the Lord Jesus over those who had evil spirits, saying, "I adjure you by the Jesus whom Paul proclaims." Seven sons of a Jewish high priest named Sceva were doing this. But the evil spirit said to them in reply, "Jesus I know, and Paul I know; but who are you?"

*Then the man with the evil spirit leaped on them,
mastered them all, and so overpowered them that they fled
out of the house naked and wounded. When this became
known to all residents of Ephesus, both Jews and Greeks,
everyone was awestruck; and the name of the Lord Jesus
was praised.*[1]

In this situation, the Apostle Paul was working in
partnership with God to accomplish the Lord's will in
his life. Saint Paul was an authentic Christian who had
an encounter with Jesus on the road to Damascus, and
after surrendering his life into the Lord's service, Paul
was baptized and received the gifts of the Holy Spirit.
When the Apostle Paul issued a command to a demonic
spirit, the power wasn't coming from Paul, it was coming directly from God, who was working in partnership
with Paul.

When the traveling Jewish exorcists tried using the
name of Jesus to cast demonic spirits out of a person,
the demons immediately recognized that those men
were *not* Christians. The Jewish exorcists had never
surrendered their lives to Jesus. They had never been
filled with the Holy Spirit. The Jewish exorcists were
not working in partnership with God. Because the
demonic spirits could sense that the power of God was
not present in their lives, they filled the possessed man
with superhuman strength, and after the possessed man
attacked the Jewish exorcists, *they fled out of the house
naked and wounded.*[2]

To answer the question of who has authority over
demonic spirits, the correct answer is God, but a more
precise answer is only an authentic Christian who is
working in partnership with God has the ability to take
authority over demonic spirits. The power and authority

over demonic spirits does not come from humans, but only from God, through the name, power and authority of Jesus, who is at work in the lives of his followers.

A good Scripture passage demonstrating an authentic Christian's power over demonic spirits comes from the Great Commission where Jesus said, *"Go into all the world and proclaim the good news to the whole creation. The one who believes and is baptized will be saved; but the one who does not believe will be condemned. And these signs will accompany those who believe: by using my name they will cast out demons; they will speak in new tongues; they will pick up snakes in their hands, and if they drink any deadly thing, it will not hurt them; they will lay their hands on the sick, and they will recover."*[3]

Another source that verifies an authentic Christian's authority over demonic spirits comes from the leading exorcist in Rome, Father Gabriele Amorth. In one of Father Amorth's books, *An Exorcist Tells His Story,* he wrote a chapter entitled "Who Can Expel Demons?" In this chapter Father Amorth says, *"I believe that I have made it sufficiently clear that Jesus gave the power to expel demons to all those who believe in him and act in his name."*[4]

In addition to all the examples that Father Amorth describes in his writings, another passage of Scripture that describes our authority over evil spirits comes from Luke 9:1–2, when *Jesus called the twelve together and gave them power and authority over all demons and to cure diseases, and he sent them out to proclaim the kingdom of God and to heal.* The power and authority that Jesus gave to the Apostles can be compared to the power given to the priesthood. According to the Catechism in section 1548, every priest receives power to drive out demons, to cure the sick and to preach the Good News through the laying on of hands at his ordination.

We also see in the Gospel of Luke 10:17–19 that Jesus sent forth seventy more disciples with the same mission. When this group returned from their first missionary assignment, they proclaimed with great joy, *"Lord, in your name even the demons submit to us!" He said to them, "I watched Satan fall from heaven like a flash of lightning. See, I have given you authority to tread on snakes and scorpions, and over all the power of the enemy; and nothing will hurt you."*

The power to take authority over evil has already been given to the Lord's disciples. It was first given to the twelve Apostles when they were sent forth in Luke 9:1–2, and then it was given to the rest of the Lord's followers in Luke 10:17–19, when the seventy were sent forth. This power comes from the Holy Spirit, and it's imparted to each believer during Baptism and Confirmation.

Another common misconception is that only a priest can say deliverance prayers. This statement also needs further clarification. According to the Catechism in section 1673, only a priest with the permission of his bishop can perform an *official exorcism*. A good example of a man who needed an official exorcism comes from the possessed man who lived among the tombs.

In Mark 5:2–8, when Jesus had *stepped out of the boat, immediately a man out of the tombs with an unclean spirit met him. He lived among the tombs; and no one could restrain him any more, even with a chain; for he had often been restrained with shackles and chains, but the chains he wrenched apart, and the shackles he broke in pieces; and no one had the strength to subdue him.*

Night and day among the tombs and on the mountains he was always howling and bruising himself with stones. When he saw Jesus from a distance, he ran and bowed down before him; and he shouted at the top of his voice, "What have you to do with me, Jesus, Son of the Most High God? I adjure you by God, do not torment me." For he had said to him, "Come out of the man, you unclean spirit!"

In this situation, the man who lived among the tombs was possessed by a legion of demons that had given him supernatural strength to rip apart chains. The demons had control over the man's behaviors and could even speak to other people using the man's voice. Because a legion of demons was in full control, the man would be classified by the Catholic Church as fully possessed and would need to undergo an official exorcism.

According to the Catechism in section 1673, *The solemn exorcism, called a major exorcism, can be performed only by a priest and with the permission of the bishop.*

Another type of demonic attack is called *oppression.* A good example of oppression comes from a man who made a sinful agreement with a demonic spirit of lust while viewing pornography on the Internet. If the man with the pornography addiction wanted to stop, but found himself constantly driven by a spiritual force outside of his control, then it would be a good indicator of demonic oppression. The man with the pornography addiction would *not* be totally possessed by evil, and he wouldn't need an official exorcism. Rather the man with the pornography addiction would need to break all sinful agreements that he made with the devil using his personal deliverance prayers, and after breaking those agreements, he would need to receive the Sacrament of Reconciliation.

In both of these situations, demonic spirits would be involved in the men's lives. The fully possessed man who lived among the tombs would need an official exorcism by an experienced priest. During the exorcism, the priest would recite special prayers from the Rite of Exorcism. For example, in one of the prayers the priest would say, *"O God, Creator and Defender of the human race, Who hast formed man in thine image, look down with pity upon this thy servant, N. (thy handmaid, N.), for he (she) has fallen a prey to the craftiness of an evil spirit.*[5] Because these prayers are specifically designed for an exorcism, a priest should only use them while casting demonic spirits out of a fully possessed person.

The difference between the prayers used in the Rite of Exorcism and personal deliverance prayers is that during an official exorcism a priest is commanding evil spirits out of a possessed person, while personal deliverance prayers are used to command evil spirits out of a person's own life and sphere of influence. Because the man with the pornography addiction would *not* be totally possessed by evil, he would still have control over his actions. Although this man may be under serious demonic attack by forces that are constantly tempting him to view more pornographic images, he could still use his free will to resist the devil.

Because demonic spirits would be inside his house, tempting him to commit a sin, the man would have the right to command those demonic spirits out of his life using the name, power and authority of Jesus. If the man with the pornography addiction were truly serious about repenting of his sin and turning his life over to Jesus, then the Lord would honor his prayers for deliverance. Upon receiving the man's act of contrition, along with his prayers commanding the demonic spirits out of his life, the Lord would send an assignment of angels to bind up and remove the demonic spirits.

Because the man with the pornography addiction made agreements with demonic spirits through his sin of lust, he would be the *only* person who would have the authority to break those agreements. A priest would *not* have the right to break sinful agreements on the man's behalf, because the priest didn't make those agreements. A priest could pray for the man's salvation and sanctification process, but he would not have the right to take authority over the demonic spirits that were outside of his sphere of influence.

As soon as the man with the pornography addiction made sinful agreements with demonic spirits, those spirits would have the right to enter his life. Because the man made those agreements, he would be the only person that would have the right to break those agreements, and once those agreements were broken, the demonic spirits would need to leave the man alone. If the demonic spirits didn't leave the man alone, he could use his personal deliverance prayers to drive the demons out of his life and sphere of influence.

Another topic that would be helpful to address would be a person's *sphere of influence*. When a priest has been assigned the role of pastor over a parish, the entire church property would fall under his sphere of influence. For example, if a demonic spirit entered the church building during Mass and started creating a disturbance, the priest would have the right to take authority over the spiritual atmosphere of the parish and command the demonic spirit to get off the property.

Other areas under a priest's sphere of influence would be his own thoughts and actions, along with any parishioner who submitted to his authority during a spiritual direction session. For example, if a man who used to perform satanic rituals scheduled an appointment with a priest for a spiritual direction session, and if during the session a demonic spirit began interfering with the man's ability to hear and understand what the priest was saying, then the priest could take authority over the room and drive the demonic spirit off the church property.

In this situation, the priest would have authority over the room and over the ex-occult member because that person would be submitting to the priest's authority during the spiritual direction session. If there were a group of active occult members living in a house across the street from the parish, the priest would *not* have any authority over the demonic spirits that those people were openly inviting into their lives, because those occult members and the property across the street would be *outside* of the priest's sphere of influence.

If the active occult members wanted to make sinful agreements with demonic spirits through their satanic rituals, then the priest could not stop them. If the demonic spirits came onto the church property and started interfering with the priest's ministry, then the priest could take authority over his own sphere of influence and ask the Lord to send an assignment of warring angels to bind up and remove those demonic spirits.

The same dynamics would also apply to the man with the pornography addiction. A priest would *not* have the right to take authority over any demonic spirits that were driving the man's pornography addiction, because the man with the addiction would be outside of the priest's sphere of influence. If the man scheduled a spiritual direction session with the priest, the priest would have the right to take authority over any demons that were interfering with the meeting, but as soon as the meeting was over, demonic spirits would have the right to tempt the man to look at more pornographic images.

The only way for the man to break free from his pornography addiction would be to take authority over his own sphere of influence, which would include his thoughts, words, actions, living space and environment. In the event that the man had small children living with him, then his children would also fall under his sphere of influence. If the man were married, his wife would also have partial authority over her husband, because the demonic spirits would be interfering with the sanctity of her marriage.

Because the man with the pornography addiction would not be classified as *possessed* by the Catholic Church, a priest could not perform an official exorcism. Because the man with the pornography addiction would be outside of the priest's sphere of influence, a priest would not have any right to take authority over the demonic spirits that were influencing his behaviors. The only way for the man with the pornography addiction to break free from demonic oppression would be to repent of his sins and use his personal deliverance prayers to drive the devil out of his life.

The same dynamics would also apply to our own lives and situations. In the event that a man or woman is fully possessed by demonic spirits, that person's friends or family members could request an official exorcism from the Catholic Church.

In the event that a man or woman is not fully possessed, that person's *only* options would be to break all sinful agreements with evil, visit the Sacrament of Reconciliation, and drive the devil out of his or her life and sphere of influence in the name, power and authority of Jesus.

Once you learn how to drive the devil out of your own life and sphere of influence, you can then help other people using the same dynamics of spiritual warfare.

COMMUNICATING WITH DEMONIC SPIRITS

Although the Bible mentions the word *ghost* several times, it is very rare that a person's soul is allowed to cross from the abode of the dead to visit the living. A good example of a time when God allowed a person's soul to deliver a message to the living comes from the life of King Saul.

According to 1 Samuel 28:3, after the prophet Samuel died, *Saul had expelled the mediums and the wizards from the land.* But when Saul found himself surrounded by the Philistine army, *he was afraid, and his heart trembled greatly.*[1]

Because God had already rejected Saul as king, his life was devoid of the Holy Spirit's guidance. Even when Saul prayed and sought guidance, *the Lord did not answer him, not by dreams, or by Urim, or by prophets.*[2] Because King Saul was desperate to hear from the Lord, he said to his servants, *"Seek out for me a woman who is a medium, so that I may go to her and inquire of her."*

His servants said to him, "There is a medium at Endor."

So Saul disguised himself and put on other clothes and went there, he and two men with him. They came to the woman by night. And he said, "Consult a spirit for me, and bring up for me the one whom I name to you."

The woman said to him, "Surely you know what Saul has done, how he has cut off the mediums and the wizards from the land. Why then are you laying a snare for my life to bring about my death?"[3]

Saul swore to her saying, *"As the Lord lives, no punishment shall come upon you for this thing."*

Then the woman said, "Whom shall I bring up for you?"

He answered, "Bring up Samuel for me."[4]

Although the Bible doesn't offer any details about the séance that occurred, one option would be the typical setting where the participants sit around a table and hold hands. Maybe the woman's house was totally dark except for one flickering candle in the center of the table. Other options would include using objects such as a crystal ball, or a scrying mirror with a flat black surface, or even a voodoo-type ceremony where the participants invite Loa spirits into their bodies.

Regardless of the type of séance that occurred, shortly after making contact with the spirit realm, the woman cried out with a loud voice and said, *"Why have you deceived me? You are Saul!"*

The king said to her, "Have no fear; what do you see?"

The woman said to Saul, "I see a divine being coming up out of the ground."

He said to her, "What is his appearance?"

She said, "An old man is coming up; he is wrapped in a robe." So Saul knew that it was Samuel, and he bowed with his face to the ground, and did obeisance.

Then Samuel said to Saul, "Why have you disturbed me by bringing me up?"

Saul answered, "I am in great distress, for the Philistines are warring against me, and God has turned away from me and answers me no more, either by prophets or by dreams; so I have summoned you to tell me what I should do."

Samuel said, "Why then do you ask me, since the Lord has turned from you and become your enemy? The Lord has done to you just as he spoke by me; for the Lord has torn the kingdom out of your hand, and given it to your neighbor, David. Moreover the Lord will give Israel along with you into the hands of the Philistines; and tomorrow you and your sons shall be with me; the Lord will also give the army of Israel into the hands of the Philistines."

Immediately Saul fell full length on the ground, filled with fear because of the words of Samuel; and there was no strength in him, for he had eaten nothing all day and all night.[5]

In this situation, the woman was able to use her psychic powers to communicate with a spirit from the dead. The problem with communicating with ghosts or seeking oracles from the dead is that you don't know what type of spiritual entity you are dealing with. Because the words of Samuel were fulfilled the following day when Saul and his sons were killed in battle, we can assume that God allowed Samuel to deliver a prophetic message from the abode of the dead.

Another possibility is that demonic spirits were impersonating the prophet Samuel by appearing in the form of an old man wrapped in a long robe. Because it's not possible to identify the source of the message, it's not wise to trust any type of message derived from spirit guide channeling. In addition to being unwise, all forms of occult practices have been defined in Sacred Scripture as a very serious sin and an open door for demonic oppression.

According to Deuteronomy 18:10–12, God said, *"No one shall be found among you who makes a son or daughter pass through fire, or who practices divination, or is a soothsayer, or an augur, or a sorcerer, or one who casts spells, or who consults ghosts or spirits, or who seeks oracles from the dead. For whoever does these things is abhorrent to the Lord."*

Even though King Saul knew it was wrong to seek oracles from the dead, because he was desperate to receive wisdom and insight concerning his situation, he violated the Lord's commandment and committed a serious sin. Even though King Saul maintained an external practice of religion by frequently invoking the name of the Lord, his heart was far from God. Because God had rejected Saul as king, his life was devoid of the Holy Spirit's guidance and he became very desperate. We can see Saul's desperation during the séance when he said, *"God has turned away from me and answers me no more, either by prophets or by dreams."[6]*

Although King Saul had an authentic desire to hear from the Lord, because of his sins of idolatry, rebellion and disobedience, God would no longer interact with him, causing an even greater emptiness inside his heart. Instead of repenting, changing his ways and turning back to God, Saul continued invoking the name of the Lord, and at the same time, seeking after false gods.

Another problem with committing the sin of idolatry, consulting ghosts or seeking oracles from the dead is that once you make contact with demonic spirits, it's impossible (without God's assistance) to get rid of them. Once a person makes contact with demonic spirits, they have the right to visit that person anytime they want. For example, in King Saul's situation, the demonic spirits that were present during the séance could have followed him into battle the next day.

Because King Saul had violated God's laws and made an agreement with demonic spirits by requesting information from the spirit realm, those demons would have the right to offer him direction and insight any time they wanted. If the demonic spirits could see several archers hiding behind a distant hillside, they may whisper thoughts into Saul's mind prompting him to head straight into danger. Or if it was in the demons' interest to protect Saul, so that they could use him to accomplish an even greater purpose in the future, they may tell him to turn back so that he could avoid the archers.

As it turns out, according to 1 Samuel 31:3–5, *the battle pressed hard upon Saul; the archers found him, and he was badly wounded by them. Then Saul said to his armor-bearer, "Draw your sword and thrust me through with it, so that these uncircumcised may not come and thrust me through, and make sport of me." But his armor-bearer was unwilling; for he was terrified. So Saul took his own sword and fell upon it. When his armor-bearer saw that Saul was dead, he also fell upon his sword and died with him.*

Another example of seeking oracles from the dead comes from the modern-day phenomena of haunted houses. The problem with the modern-day haunted house theory is that once a person dies, their soul is *not* free to take up residence inside an abandoned building, or to stalk people in the subway, or wander around the neighborhood late at night. When a person dies, their soul goes directly to God for judgment. According to the Catechism in section 1022, *each man receives his eternal retribution in his immortal soul at the very moment of his death.*

Because God is all knowing and all powerful over our afterlife existence, it would not be possible to escape his judgment or remain behind on earth even for a second—unless, of course, it was within his divine will. Usually in the case of so-called haunted houses, the occupants of the property have committed the sin of idolatry and have given demonic spirits the right to interfere with their lives.

Once the sin of idolatry has been committed, it will be impossible (without God's assistance) to make them leave. Because demonic spirits only have one purpose, *to steal and kill and destroy,*[7] they will disguise their true identity and appear in the form of helpless little children. That way, the occupants of the property will think that a person has been trapped inside the house and needs their help. Demonic spirits will use this tactic because they want to open up lines of communication with the occupants in an attempt to develop a strong-hold and drive them deeper into bondage.

Other times demonic spirits will create creepy scratching noises from inside the walls in an attempt to cause fear and harass the occupants. In one situation, a Christian pastor was raising three teenage children in his two-story home, and even though the pastor and his wife never experienced any kind of demonic activity, all three of his children reported seeing an obscure old man late at night. As it turns out, the teenagers were also involved with a make-believe form of magic spell casting after reading the Harry Potter books.

Although reading a Harry Potter book may seem innocent enough, all it would take to open a line of communication with demonic spirits would be a simple desire. If the teenagers wanted to be like Harry Potter so that they could communicate with spirit guides, receive hidden knowledge or possess supernatural powers to protect themselves, then those desires would be enough to offer demonic spirits an invitation into the pastor's home.

The same invitation would occur if the teenagers were playing with an Ouija board in the basement. If the teenagers turned off all the lights and started asking the spirit realm questions, then demonic spirits would have the right to speak to those participants. If the teenagers took hold of the pendulum and asked the spirit guides to spell out answers to their questions, they may even feel their hands moving across the board as the pendulum identified different letters and numbers.

After the teenagers' playtime was over, the demonic spirits wouldn't leave the pastor's home and go down the street to seduce other children. Once demonic spirits have been invited into a person's life through the sin of idolatry, witchcraft, divination, spirit guide channeling or seeking oracles from the dead, they will remain there until they are forced to leave.

BUILDING A SPIRITUAL CANOPY AROUND YOUR HOME

In the event that you have been experiencing some kind of demonic activity inside your home, the first step to remove those intruders would be to acknowledge the truth. Is there really a helpless little child trapped in between time dimensions that needs your help, or have you or one of your family members committed the sin of idolatry through spirit guide channeling or seeking oracles from the dead? Is there really an obscure old man visiting your children late at night, or have they been reading Harry Potter books, communicating with spirit guides and casting spells?

In the event that you or your family members have been experiencing any kind of supernatural phenomena inside your home, you can use the following steps to drive the demonic intruders out of your life and sphere of influence in the name, power and authority of Jesus.

Step 1: Conduct a Family Bible Study
The first step in removing demonic intruders from your home would be to conduct a family Bible study. Because it will *not* be possible to repent of the sin of idolatry without first understanding why it is wrong, it would be helpful to set aside some time to carefully examine Sacred Scripture. Because there are over fifty references to the words *demons* and *demonic* in the New Testament, it would be helpful for every family member to present a teaching on one of those Scripture passages. Other options for a family Bible study would include a deeper examination of the words *idol* or *idolatry*.

Step 2: Make a Complete Act of Contrition

After all your family members understand why the sin of idolatry harms your relationship with God, the next step would be to search your past and make a complete act of contrition. Maybe one of your family members committed the sin of idolatry ten years ago and has forgotten all about the experience. For example, maybe your spouse participated in a voodoo ceremony while celebrating at Mardi Gras in New Orleans, or paid a psychic healer a few dollars for a palm reading at the county fair. Even if nothing paranormal occurred at the time, if that person exhibited a desire to engage in any kind of communication with the spiritual realm (other than to God), then demonic spirits would have the right to fulfill that request at any time, even ten years later inside your home.

Step 3: Renounce the Sin of Idolatry

After all the sins of idolatry, fortune-telling, palm reading, divination, occult practices and witchcraft have been identified, the next step would be to acknowledge those actions as sinful and confess them to the Lord. In the event that your children have been reading Harry Potter books, casting spells or playing with the Ouija board in the basement, ask your children to renounce those actions and confess them as sinful during your family prayer session.

If you or your spouse have visited a psychic healer or have participated in the New Age movement, break those agreements in the name, power and authority of Jesus. If all your family members are Catholic, it would be helpful to bring those sins to the Sacrament of Reconciliation. In the event that your family members are not Catholic, you can apply a passage of Scripture to your life from James 5:16, that says, *confess your sins to one another, and pray for one another, so that you may be healed.*

Step 4: Identify Objects of Witchcraft

After all your family members have searched their hearts for any kind of open doors to the demonic, the next step would be to search your house to identify any objects of witchcraft. In the event that your children have been reading Harry Potter books or playing with tarot cards or the Ouija board, it will be necessary to remove those items from the property. If your spouse has been using a talisman, amulet or any other type of ritually charged object for good luck or supernatural protection, then deep in that person's heart they have been committing the sin of idolatry. Instead of turning to God for protection, they are asking unknown spiritual forces for help. Anytime a person asks unknown spiritual forces for help, demonic spirits would have the right to interfere with that person's life.

The process of searching through every item in your home may take some time. It may be necessary to go through all the boxes in the attic and basement. One woman named Deborah had several boxes of witchcraft supplies in her crawl space. Even though Deborah had been a Christian for many years, she continued holding onto parts of her past where she participated in a witch's coven. Even though Deborah had repented of her witchcraft sins, she was still holding onto the medicine bag and photographs of her old witch friends. Even though Deborah had forgotten about the boxes in her crawl space, demonic spirits could still access her life through those objects.

After the Holy Spirit identified the boxes in Deborah's crawl space as the source of the attack, she still had a hard time removing them from her property. That's because deep in Deborah's heart she still had soul-ties to all her old witch friends. Deborah had to struggle for several weeks before being set free. In order to break free, Deborah needed to search her heart and make a decision: Would she continue holding onto her past life as a witch, or would she completely trust Jesus with her heart?

In the event that you find some questionable objects inside your home, it would be helpful to examine your heart to study what attracted you to those objects in the first place. For example, if you have a box of New Age crystals in the basement, are those stones part of a larger rock collection, or do they provide spiritual power and protection? If you have a dream catcher on the wall, is it simply a form of decoration, or does it capture supernatural power to influence your dreams?

Step 5: Destroy Any Objects of Witchcraft

After your family members have searched the entire house, it may to helpful to conduct another prayer meeting before removing any questionable objects from the property. For example, if your husband has a collection of pornographic magazines in the basement, you could ask him to denounce all forms of sexual immorality and burn those magazines in the fireplace. Other objects of witchcraft such as talismans, amulets and good luck charms could be destroyed with a hammer before throwing them in the trash. While these items are being destroyed, it would be helpful for your family members to denounce all sinful agreements with demonic spirits in the name, power and authority of Jesus.

Step 6: Dedicate Your Property to God

After you have destroyed and removed any objects of witchcraft from your home, the next step would be to dedicate your property to the Blessed Trinity. Your home should be a purified spiritual environment similar to a church. You should never allow any kind of sinful activity to enter your home. It should be a sacred sanctuary for you, your family members and the Blessed Trinity, completely free and clean of any demonic activity.

The best way to dedicate your property to the Lord is through prayer. All you need to do is gather your family members together and ask the Lord to descend upon your property with the power of the Holy Spirit to drive out and destroy any demonic intruders. It may be helpful to mark the sign of the cross on all doors and windows using anointing oil. Another option would be to establish a perimeter around the property using holy water or blessed salt. It would also be possible to drive wooden stakes into the ground at all four corners, and then mark those stakes with anointing oil.

The purpose of establishing a perimeter around the property (with anointed rocks, stakes or holy water) is to declare to the spirit realm that your property belongs to God—that your home, family members and every piece of personal property inside the home has been dedicated to God for the purpose of his glory, and that no demonic trespassers are allowed.

Step 7: Destroy Any Demonic Trespassers

After you have dedicated your property to the Blessed Trinity and established an impenetrable spiritual canopy around the perimeter, the next step would be to enforce your rights by asking Jesus to destroy any demonic trespassers. You can accomplish this step through ongoing prayer by asking Jesus to post *no trespassing* signs in the spirit realm. Once your property has been consecrated to the Lord (meaning that no form of sin or demonic activity is ever allowed on the property), then all you need to do is ask God to send an assignment of warring angels to strike down and destroy any trespassing demons.

If a demonic spirit appears as a lost, helpless little child, simply command it to get off your property in the name, power and authority of Jesus. If it doesn't obey, ask Jesus to send an assignment of warring angels to strike down and destroy the entire principality where the demon came from. Once you build an impenetrable spiritual canopy around your home, and maintain it with a zero-tolerance policy, you will never again experience another ghost-like phenomena inside your home.

DENOUNCING THE SIN OF DIVINATION

The sin of divination occurs when a person turns to fallen angels to obtain information about the future, instead of turning to God in prayer. A good example of how the sin of divination works comes from a slave girl in the Acts of the Apostles. When Saint Paul and his companions were ministering in Philippi, they *met a slave-girl who had a spirit of divination and brought her owners a great deal of money by fortune-telling.*[1]

In this situation, a demonic spirit had entered the slave girl's life through the sin of fortune-telling. Once a demonic spirit had developed an intimate relationship with the slave girl, it would give her information about the future. For example, if a man came to the slave girl and paid for her fortune-telling services, the girl would make an inquiry into the spiritual realm. Upon receiving this request, the demonic spirits that had been assigned to the slave girl would communicate with the demonic spirits that had been assigned to the man.

Because the demonic spirits that followed the man around would have intimate details about his life that no other person would know, the demons could communicate that information to the slave girl. Upon receiving the man's personal information, the slave girl could deliver a message to the man that the demons wanted him to hear. Upon receiving this message, the man would be astounded that a slave girl, who he had never met before, could know so many personal details about his life.

Because the slave girl was very good at listening to the seductive and alluring voices of the demonic spirits, she was able to make *her owners a great deal of money by fortune-telling.*[2] Although the slave girl and the demonic spirits were able to work together in partnership to advance Satan's kingdom, they made a terrible mistake when they interfered with Saint Paul's ministry.

According to Acts 16:17–18, the slave girl began following Paul and his companions, crying out with a loud voice saying, *"These men are slaves of the Most High God, who proclaim to you a way of salvation." She kept doing this for many days. But Paul, very much annoyed, turned and said to the spirit, "I order you in the name of Jesus Christ to come out of her." And it came out that very hour.*

After Saint Paul had cast a demonic spirit out of the slave girl, it appeared that she had lost her ability to communicate with the spirit realm. *When her owners saw that their hope of making money was gone, they seized Paul and Silas and dragged them into the marketplace before the authorities. The crowd joined in attacking them, and the magistrates had them stripped of their clothing and ordered them to be beaten with rods.*[3]

Although it may have appeared the slave girl lost her ability to communicate with the spirit realm, the demons may have been playing dead because they wanted to cause problems for Paul and his companions. Another option was that Paul prayed for an assignment of warring angels to strike down and destroy the demonic spirits that were driving the slave girl's behavior.

If that were the case, God's angelic warriors would have cut the demons into pieces and sealed their remains in the lake of fire. If Paul had asked God to completely destroy the demonic spirits, instead of just commanding them into the abyss, the slave girl would have temporarily lost her fortune-telling abilities, but in order to get them back, all she would need to do is make more agreements with demonic spirits of divination through the sin of idolatry.

Another option was that after Paul cast a spirit of fortune-telling out of the slave girl, one of his companions took the time to present the Gospel message to her. Upon receiving the Good News, the slave girl may have accepted Jesus as her Savior, and in doing so, she would have transitioned out of the kingdom of darkness and into the light. If this were the case, the slave girl would have been filled with the power of the Holy Spirit, and at that point, the owners would have lost all hopes of making money through her fortune-telling abilities.

Because all forms of divination involve communication with demonic spirits, you may want to study the following list to see if you have ever participated in any of these activities. In the event that you have committed the sin of divination, take a moment right now to denounce the practice of _____ in the name, power and authority of Jesus. After denouncing all forms of divination, spend some time breaking all the agreements that you made with demonic spirits using the prayer at the end of this chapter.

Astrology — Is a belief that the positions of stars and planets are useful for providing information about a person's life. Instead of turning to God for direction, answers and insight, people who follow the zodiac (or who read horoscopes) are using the constellations as a form of fortune-telling.

Automatic Writing — Is a New Age technique where a person enters a demonic trance and writes down messages from the spirit realm.

Clairvoyance — Is the ability to see into the spirit realm or to communicate by visual images. The ability to hear in the spirit realm or to communicate by mental thoughts is called *clairaudience*.

Numerology — A form of divination where the value of numbers or letters is used to interpret the mystical readings about a person's life.

Ouija Board — A board game used to communicate with spirit guides. After asking the netherworld a question, the participants place their hands on a pointer and allow demonic spirits to guide their hands around the board in an attempt to highlight specific letters and numbers that spell out answers to their questions.

Pendulum — A pendulum is any kind of swinging object that is used for divination. If the demonic forces swing the pendulum clockwise, one interpretation is given; if the pendulum moves counter-clockwise, a different interpretation is perceived.

Psychic Readings — Occur when a person visits a fortune-teller, medium or seer who communicates with the spirit realm. During these sessions the fortune-teller may interpret lines or patterns on a person's hand; or they may gaze into a crystal ball, or even drop melting wax or pebbles into a pool of water to interpret the ebb and flow.

Spirit Guide Channeling — An occult practice where a person invites demonic spirits into his or her life in the form of spirit guides for the purpose of receiving messages and insight.

Stichomancy — Is a form of divination that works by placing a book on its spine. After the book is allowed to fall open to a random page, a person places his or her finger on the page and reads a passage as if the message was being delivered from the spirit realm.

Tarot Cards — A form of divination where a deck of seventy-eight cards are shuffled and spread out on a table using various patterns. After the participants ask the spirit realm a question, they allow demonic spirits to guide their hands when choosing a card. After a card has been chosen, an interpretation is given.

Transcendental Meditation — Is a New Age technique where a person chants the names of demonic entities as a mantra for the purpose of making contact with the spirit realm. Participants in these Hindu and Buddhist exercises are encouraged to assume a passive and accepting posture so that they can enter a trance-like state when inviting spirit guides into their lives.

Water Witching — A method of searching for underground water where a person uses two steel or copper wires (or two wooden sticks) as a form of divination. Because there is no scientific reason for wooden sticks or copper wires to move on their own accord in the presence of water, the powers behind this practice are considered to be from the demonic.

In the event that you have participated in any of these forms of divination, you can use the following prayer to denounce those practices in the name, power and authority of Jesus.

Dear Heavenly Father, in the name of your only begotten Son, Jesus Christ, I denounce Satan and all his works, all forms of witchcraft, the use of divination, the practice of sorcery, dealing with mediums, channeling with spirit guides, the Ouija board, astrology, Reiki, hypnosis, automatic writing, horoscopes, numerology, all types of fortune-telling, palm reading, levitation and anything else associated with the occult or Satan.

I denounce and forsake my involvement in all of them in the name of Jesus Christ who came in the flesh, and by the power of his cross, his blood and his resurrection, I break their hold over my life. I confess all these sins before you, and ask you to cleanse and forgive me.

I ask you Lord Jesus to enter my heart and create in me the kind of person you have intended me to be. I ask you to send forth the gifts of your Holy Spirit to baptize me, just as you baptized your disciples on the day of Pentecost. I thank you Heavenly Father for strengthening my inner spirit with the power of your Holy Spirit, so that Christ may dwell in my heart. Amen.

TALISMANS, AMULETS & GOOD LUCK CHARMS

A talisman or amulet is an object that attracts, channels and directs demonic powers. These objects are often used as good luck charms and come in a variety of different forms, including pendants with satanic images, rings, stones and coins. Even a religious icon, a statue of Saint Joseph or a lucky rabbit's foot can be used to channel spiritual powers. These objects are often acquired for the purpose of selling real estate, attracting wealth and romance into a person's life, or providing protection from accidents, illness and death.

A good example of a talisman comes from a man from Pakistan named Hammad who went to a witch doctor to purchase a ritually charged object. Hammad wanted a talisman that would protect him from death. After paying the witch doctor a large sum of money, an artist created a silver pendant with satanic symbols. After the witch doctor attached a black rope, he conducted a satanic ritual to assign demonic spirits of protection to the object.

When Hammad went to pick up his talisman, he was very impressed with the artistic design. Although he liked how the pendant looked, he wanted to make sure it would protect him from death. To test the spiritual powers of this object, Hammad purchased a live chicken from the local market, and after gathering a few of his friends together, he drove to the edge of town. Upon arriving at their destination, Hammad tied the pendant around the chicken's neck and placed the chicken fifty feet away in a rocky outcrop surrounded by tall grass.

One by one, the men took turns firing bullets at the chicken. After the first shot rang out, Hammad was amazed that the chicken was still alive. When his best friend fired the rifle, the bird didn't even move. After the third, fourth and fifth shots were fired, Hammad was very impressed with the talisman's spiritual power. Because the men wanted to eat the chicken for lunch, they removed the pendant from the bird's neck, and were finally able to kill the chicken.

One possibility for the chicken's ability to survive for so long was that the demonic spirits that had been assigned to the talisman by the witch doctor were deflecting the bullets in midair. Another possibility was that demonic spirits were interfering with the men's vision or with their ability to properly aim their firearms. Another possibility was that Hammad's friends didn't want to kill the chicken, because they knew how much money he paid the witch doctor.

Although we may never know what took place in the spirit realm concerning the chicken's ability to survive several bullets, we do know that when Hammad accepted the talisman, he made an agreement with demonic spirits. When Hammad placed the talisman around his neck, he said to the spirit realm, "I want your protection. I give you permission to interact with my life."

The problem with making these kinds of agreements with demonic spirits is that fallen angels only have one purpose, *to steal and kill and destroy.*[1] Although demonic spirits may appear to be friendly by offering their victims some kind of benefit, such as information about the future or protection from harm, they can never be trusted. The same demonic entities that may have helped the chicken survive several bullets can also cause divorce, mysterious forms of illness and accidents to occur.

Once these demonic spirits develop a stronghold in Hammad's life, they will never leave him alone. They will constantly drive him deeper into bondage, using his life as a pawn to advance Satan's kingdom. Even if Hammad traveled to a different country, far away from the principality where the witch doctor's demons reside, other demonic entities in that area could still access Hammad's life through the talisman that was tied around his neck.

The only way for Hammad to break free would be to cancel all the vows and agreements that he made with the demonic spirits. Hammad would also need to accept Jesus as the Lord of his life. He would need to confess the sin of using talismans, amulets and good luck charms. Instead of turning to demonic entities for protection, Hammad would need to offer that place deep within his heart to the Blessed Trinity.

It would also be necessary for Hammad to destroy any talismans, amulets and good luck charms, especially those with demonic symbols, and completely remove them from his life and environment. When an object has been created for the purpose of evil, it cannot be cleansed through prayer, but needs to be destroyed.

INVOKING SPIRITUAL POWERS FOR SELLING REAL ESTATE

Another example of a talisman comes from a clear plastic tube that contains a statue of Saint Joseph. Although Saint Joseph is considered to be a good and holy saint, the plastic figurine that is being marketed in *home sales kits* becomes an object similar to a talisman because it has been created for the purpose of involving supernatural powers for selling real estate.

According to the home sale kit instructions, the statue needs to be buried upside down in the ground. Condo owners are encouraged to bury the statue in a flowerpot. Other sources insist the statue needs to be buried near the real estate sign. Some people bury Saint Joseph laying on his back with his head pointing toward the house to create a type of *magnetic arrow*. The purpose of the magnetic arrow is to draw potential buyers to the property and to influence the buyer's decision into signing a full-price contract.

In the spirit realm, there are only two possible options for this situation. One option is that whenever the real Saint Joseph looks down from heaven and sees a man burying a plastic statue in the ground with his image, he goes before God's throne and intercedes on that person's behalf. Maybe Saint Joseph would speak to God by saying, "Please bring a full-priced offer for Scott's property. I know that Scott doesn't maintain an authentic relationship with you, and that he doesn't want to make you Lord of his life, or even Lord of his financial affairs, but please, let's sell his home in one day so that my home sales kit gets all the credit."

The other option in this situation is that demonic spirits would look down upon the property and see a clear plastic tube with a statue of Saint Joseph inside. Because the tube had been buried in such a way as to create a *magnetic arrow to invoke supernatural powers for the purpose of selling real estate,* the demons would know that Scott was open to receiving spiritual assistance from any kind of spiritual entity that would give him whatever he wanted.

Upon receiving this invitation, the demons would have the right to start interacting with Scott in a way that seemed most helpful. If it were in the demons' advantage to influence Scott's decision to lower the price, they may interfere with his thoughts. If it were in the demons' advantage to draw Scott deeper into bondage, or to make him angry with God because his house didn't sell fast enough, they would have that right, all because Scott buried a talisman in his front yard and extended an invitation for spiritual assistance.

Not only is the home sales kit an open door for demonic influence, but it would also rob Scott of the opportunity to make Jesus the Lord of his life. Jesus wants to develop a deep and intimate relationship with all of his beloved children. Jesus wants all of his followers to seek his guidance and learn how to listen to his softly spoken voice. Because Jesus has a purpose and plan for Scott's life, it would be important for Scott to spend time in prayer, asking Jesus questions about his finances.

For example, maybe it would be in Scott's interest to remain in his home because Jesus could foresee an economic turndown on the horizon. If it wasn't in Scott's interest to buy a larger, more expensive house, he could ask Jesus a simple question by saying, "Do you want me to sell my three-bedroom house and buy a five-bedroom home? Yes or no?" If Jesus said *no,* because of the impending economic turndown, then Scott would need to trust in the Lord and be obedient.

Or maybe Jesus could see that it was the top of the real estate market, and that it would be in Scott's interest to sell his three-bedroom home and rent a condo for the next several years. If this were the case, Scott could ask the Lord a simple question by saying, "Do you want me to sell my house and rent a condo? Yes or no?" If Jesus gave his permission to sell the home, Scott could proceed with confidence knowing that Jesus would work in partnership with him to accomplish his will in his life.

By making Jesus the Lord of his life, Scott wouldn't need to bury a talisman in his front yard. Through a serious prayer life and an authentic relationship with the Blessed Trinity, Scott could ask the Lord any questions that he wanted about his life, and after resting in Sacred Silence of a contemplative prayer life, he could discern the Lord's answers, and receive an abundance of wisdom, knowledge and guidance.

In the event that you have been invoking supernatural powers with talismans or amulets, or turning to magic charms for blessings and protection, it would be wise to denounce those practices in the name, power and authority of Jesus. After you have denounced the use of talismans, amulets and good luck charms, and have broken all agreements with the demonic spirits that operate behind those objects, it would be helpful to search your home and environment to identify any objects of witchcraft that need to be destroyed. For example, any kind of Santeria, New Age, voodoo or black magic objects, or any kind of jewelry with demonic or satanic symbols, will need to be destroyed.

In the event that you have any charm bracelets or satanic jewelry, they will also need to be destroyed. According to the Catechism in section 2117, *wearing charms is also reprehensible.* The word *reprehensible* means being worthy of a rebuke or punishment.

Because talismans and amulets can take on many different forms, it would also be helpful to evaluate the desires of your heart to determine why you have acquired any questionable objects and brought them inside your home. Since a statue is nothing more than a piece of wood, plastic or ceramic, the statue is *not* the problem, it's the intentions and desire within a person's heart that opens the door to the demonic.

After you have identified, removed and destroyed any talismans, amulets or good luck charms, you can use the following prayer to seal the door shut.

Dear Heavenly Father, in the name of your only begotten Son, Jesus Christ, I denounce Satan and all his works, along with all forms of witchcraft, including the use of talismans, amulets and good luck charms, and anything else associated with the occult or Satan. Please forgive me for turning to religious objects, statues, icons and magic charms as a source of power and protection, instead of turning to you with all my love and devotion.

Please forgive me for wearing magic charms, and for obtaining spiritually charged objects for the purpose of attracting love and romance into my life. Please forgive me for using religious objects for the purpose of invoking supernatural powers for selling real estate. Please forgive me for using good luck charms in an attempt to channel wealth and prosperity into my life. I renounce and forsake my involvement in all these practices in the name, power and authority of Jesus.

In the name of Jesus Christ who came in the flesh, and by the power of his cross, his blood and his resurrection, I command any demonic forces that have entered my life or attached themselves to me through these sins—by the power of the Lord God Almighty, in the name of Jesus Christ my Savior—to leave me forever, and to be consigned into the everlasting lake of fire, that they may never again touch me or any other creature in the entire world. Amen.

ALCOHOL, MARIJUANA & PHARMACEUTICAL DRUGS

One day a homeless man named Fred discovered an abandoned house on the outskirts of town. Although the back door had been covered with a piece of plywood, the nails that were driven into the frame had started to rust. It didn't take long for Fred to pull away a corner of the plywood, slip his hand inside and unlock the door.

Once inside the home, Fred set up his campsite in the master bedroom located on the second floor. Because Fred was an alcoholic, he would venture out every day to hold up a cardboard sign at busy intersections for several hours that read, "Please help! Will work for food." Once Fred acquired around fifteen dollars, he would head to the nearest liquor store to buy a half-gallon of vodka.

One day while Fred was panhandling on the sidewalk outside of a popular retail store, he started getting belligerent with some of the store's customers because he wasn't receiving money fast enough. After an elderly lady complained, the store owner went outside to confront Fred. Soon a heated argument developed. Because the store owner went back inside to call the police, Fred took off running down the street.

From a physical perspective, it may appear as if these two men exchanged a few heated words and then parted ways, but from a spiritual perspective, the confrontation was under the influence of demonic spirits. Although several guardian angels had been assigned to Fred's life, there were also many demonic spirits that Fred had made agreements with over the years that were enabling his drinking problems and keeping him away from the Lord's sanctification process.

When the store owner threatened Fred's life and spoke word curses against his well-being, the demonic spirits that had been assigned to the store owner may have taken those threats as a form of permission to attack Fred. Because the demonic spirits would have the right to follow Fred back to the abandoned house, they would be able to evaluate his situation. Because Fred had broken into the building, the demons would have the right to enter the residence and manifest their powers. Because Fred was trespassing, he wouldn't be able to take authority over the building, or to build a spiritual canopy of protection around the property.

Because Fred was getting drunk for the purpose of numbing his emotions and escaping reality, the demonic spirits would have the right to interfere with his perception of reality. Because Fred was constantly rejecting the Holy Spirit's guidance, and only wanted to feel good and zone out when he was intoxicated, it opened a doorway for demonic spirits to interfere with his thoughts.

Later that evening after Fred finished drinking the rest of his vodka, demonic spirits began to influence his thoughts, making him think the house was on fire. In a fear-driven panic to save his life from the imaginary flames, Fred rushed to the second-story window and jumped outside. He landed on the concrete slab below where he fractured his leg and rendered himself unconscious. When Fred awoke the next morning in agonizing pain, he realized the house was not on fire, and that it was only his imagination.

In this situation, God wanted to prevent an accident from occurring that caused Fred to experience a permanent disability, but because Fred had opened the door to the demonic, God allowed the painful situation to occur, hoping that Fred would eventually hit bottom and change his ways. If the only way God could get Fred to stop drinking would be to allow him to experience the painful consequences of his actions, then God in his great love for Fred would allow those events to occur.

In his great love for humanity, God has made it clear in Scripture that getting intoxicated is a serious sin that will hinder our relationship with the Holy Spirit. In Galatians 5:19–21, Saint Paul says, *"Now the works of the flesh are obvious: fornication, impurity, licentiousness, idolatry, sorcery, enmities, strife, jealousy, anger, quarrels, dissensions, factions, envy, drunkenness, carousing, and things like these. I am warning you, as I warned you before: those who do such things will not inherit the kingdom of God."*

The word *licentiousness* means lacking sexual constraints or disregarding the laws of sexual morality. The word *carousing* means to take part in a drinking bout. Maybe a better definition for the word *carousing* would be all the destructive behavior that occurs in a bar after a man gets drunk.

When a man is intoxicated, the Holy Spirit is forced to depart from his life, and when the Holy Spirit departs, it leaves behind an open door for demonic spirits. Once demonic spirits begin influencing a drunk man's thoughts, they will distort his perception of reality and prompt him to do things that he wouldn't ordinarily do, including engaging in sexual immorality, anger and quarrels, along with all the other sins mentioned in Saint Paul's letter to the Galatians.

Another example of how demonic spirits have the ability to destroy a person's life when that man or woman is under the influence of alcohol, marijuana or narcotics comes from the recent Flakka epidemic that is currently sweeping across the nation. The term *Flakka* is used to describe a synthetic crystal that's more addictive and dangerous than crack cocaine. It's being imported from China in the form of bath salts because the product looks similar to white rock salt.

A small dose of this inexpensive drug will provide users with a blast of euphoria, superhuman strength and off-the-chart vital signs. It has the ability to raise a person's body temperature, heart rate and blood pressure to near-lethal levels. Shortly after taking this drug, many users start hallucinating and become extremely dangerous.

One woman named Stephanie was given this drug at a party. After a quick blast of euphoria, she found herself overwhelmed with paranoia. She thought people were watching her, so she took off running down the street. When she came to a three-story bridge, she tore off her clothes and jumped into the water. All she could remember was the feeling of being able to breath under water. She woke up in the emergency room, not knowing how she survived.

Other Flakka users have been captured on video impaling themselves on fence posts and screaming profanities while vandalizing parked cars. One man was able to overpower four police officers, and then he took off down the street running into oncoming traffic. Many of these scenes look similar to the man who was possessed by a legion of demons that *lived among the tombs; and no one could restrain him any more, even with a chain; for he had often been restrained with shackles and chains, but the chains he wrenched apart, and the shackles he broke in pieces; and no one had the strength to subdue him.*[1]

Although it may be easy to see how getting drunk and high on illegal street drugs is an open door for the demonic, it may be a little more difficult to understand why smoking cigarettes or taking doctor-prescribed psychological medications would also grieve the Holy Spirit. For example, in Fred's situation, the use of tobacco may be one of the Holy Spirit's least concerns. After Fred jumped out of the second-story window, the Holy Spirit's top priority would be to get him medical attention so that his leg would heal properly.

After Fred surrendered his life to the Lord, the Holy Spirit's next step would be to get him into a detoxification facility. After Fred stopped drinking, the Holy Spirit's next priority would be to help him find meaningful employment. If during this time Fred smoked two packs of cigarettes per day and had a constant stream of profanities flying out of his mouth, the Holy Spirit may overlook those issues for a brief time while focusing on more important problems.

If Fred accomplished everything the Holy Spirit was asking to the best of his abilities, God would be very pleased with his growth and sanctification process. In the event that Fred continued walking in partnership with God, a time would come when the Holy Spirit would confront him on the use of profanities. After Fred successfully removed profanities from his vocabulary, the Holy Spirit's next priority may be to ask him to stop smoking cigarettes.

Although smoking may have been a low priority for the Holy Spirit when Fred was getting drunk, it would eventually become more serious as Fred grew in holiness. Once the Holy Spirit started convicting Fred of a sin every time he lit up a cigarette, he would eventually have a choice to make: Would he continue walking in partnership with God and growing in holiness, or would he say *no* to God and remain stagnant? If Fred rejected the Holy Spirit's guidance, he may lose God's blessings and protection, and if Fred's rebellion continued, he may eventually find himself living back on the streets.

Because God loves Fred and is concerned for his well-being, he will not allow the sin of smoking to go on for very long. The first reason is that cigarettes are loaded with toxic chemicals that cause cancer. Because God loves Fred, he will not want to see his life cut short due to cancer. God also doesn't want to see Fred experience the painful consequences of having cancer spread through his body, or to see Fred endure the high costs and destructive side effects associated with radiation or chemotherapy treatments.

In addition to all these concerns, a compulsive need to poison the temple of the Holy Spirit is a direct violation of 1 Corinthians 6:19–20, when Saint Paul said, *"Do you not know that your body is a temple of the Holy Spirit within you, which you have from God, and that you are not your own? For you were bought with a price; therefore glorify God in your body."*

GRIEVING THE HOLY SPIRIT WITH PHARMACEUTICAL DRUGS

Another reason why God would have a problem with any type of addiction, including mood-altering psychological medications, is that they prevent a person from listening to and discerning the softly spoken voice of the Holy Spirit. Because doctor-prescribed antidepressant medications have been designed to make a person feel better, they also have the potential to repress a person's negative emotions.

Because everybody wants to feel good and no one wants to experience negative emotions, psychological medications may seem to be very helpful. For example, when Fred was getting drunk, whenever a negative feeling arose within his heart that caused him to feel bad, he would simply drink more alcohol to make himself feel better.

After Fred stopped drinking, he would be forced to deal with his past. If an onslaught of repressed emotions were too much for Fred to handle, or if demonic spirits continued to poke his festering emotional wounds plaguing him with suicidal thoughts, then taking doctor-prescribed psychological medications for a short period of time may be very helpful.

After Fred stopped drinking and surrendered his life to the Lord, the Holy Spirit would want him to resolve all of his repressed childhood issues and forgive the people who had hurt him. Because Fred had experienced many painful events during his childhood, the Holy Spirit would want him to embrace all of his hurt and surrender that hurt to God, so that God could fill his heart with his incredible love.

Because psychological medications are designed to numb out and repress a person's negative emotions, using these drugs would interfere with Fred's ability to experience painful events from his past. If Fred were prevented from embracing the pain of his past, he would not be able to complete the forgiveness process. If Fred failed to forgive the people in his past who hurt him, he would be in direct violation of the Lord's commandment in Matthew 6:14–15, where Jesus said, *"For if you forgive others their trespasses, your heavenly Father will also forgive you; but if you do not forgive others, neither will your Father forgive your trespasses."*

Because pharmaceutical companies make a lot of money convincing people that they need a never-ending supply of drugs to make themselves feel better, there's little incentive for the medical industry to cut back on anyone's prescriptions. When a patient's body becomes immune to the drugs, the doctor will usually prescribe a stronger dose. When the maximum dose is reached, and the patient has *not* dealt with the underlying source of his or her repressed emotional issues, the doctor will simply change one form of medication to a different type of medication.

Whenever any type of drug, whether it's an illegal street narcotic or a doctor-prescribed psychological medication, is used for the purpose of making a person feel better, it would fall under the sin of debauchery. The word *debauchery* means indulging in fleshly or sensual pleasures. A good example of the Bible's use for the word *debauchery* comes from Ephesians 5:18, where Saint Paul says, *"Do not get drunk with wine, for that is debauchery; but be filled with the Spirit."*

Another warning about the pursuit of sensual pleasures comes from Romans 8:5–8, where Saint Paul says, *"For those who live according to the flesh set their minds on the things of the flesh, but those who live according to the Spirit set their minds on the things of the Spirit. To set the mind on the flesh is death, but to set the mind on the Spirit is life and peace. For this reason the mind that is set on the flesh is hostile to God; it does not submit to God's law—indeed it cannot, and those who are in the flesh cannot please God."*

Because God always has our best interests at heart, it would be helpful to ask the Holy Spirit if you have ever committed the sin of debauchery by pursuing sensual pleasures. Are there any false lovers in your life that you have been turning to for pleasure and comfort instead of turning to God? Have you been turning to alcohol, marijuana or narcotics to make yourself feel better? Or is an authentic relationship with Jesus more than enough to satisfy your soul?

In the event that you have been turning to drugs or alcohol to make yourself feel better, it would be helpful to repent of those sins and ask for God's love to take that place in your heart. If you have been taking doctor-prescribed psychological medications, you may want to ask the Holy Spirit if it's time to cut back on the dosage, so that you can embrace the pain of the past, work your way through the forgiveness process, and be set free—free to be the child of God the Lord has intended you to be.

PRAYER FOR SPIRITUAL ANTABUSE

Another option for turning away from the sin of debauchery would be to pray for a strong dose of *spiritual Antabuse*. Although Antabuse is a prescription drug that is used for the treatment of alcohol addiction, it would be possible to ask God for a spiritual version of this drug to accomplish the same results.

The prescription drug Antabuse works by preventing a person's liver from breaking down acetaldehyde, a substance the body naturally produces whenever alcohol is consumed. When acetaldehyde builds up in a person's bloodstream, it produces extremely unpleasant results. The painful consequences of taking the slightest sip of alcohol while a person is on Antabuse can occur within minutes and last up to several hours.

The reaction of mixing alcohol with Antabuse is so severe that most users would rather abstain from drinking than feel profoundly sick. Because Antabuse remains active in a person's body for up to two weeks, it works as an effective deterrent to prevent recovering alcoholics from taking another drink. If a man or woman knows that the slightest sip of alcohol would make him or her feel horribly sick, then Antabuse has the ability to provide a strong motivation for that person to stay sober.

In the same way that a person can take Antabuse in an attempt to turn away from the destructive consequences of drinking, it's also possible to ask God to administer a spiritual form of this drug for almost any kind of sin imaginable. For example, if a man were struggling with a pornography addiction, it would be possible to ask God to give him a dose of spiritual Antabuse. If God took away all the pleasure that the man experienced when he looked at pornographic images, and replaced it with a painful sensation that made him feel horribly sick, then he would be highly motivated to change his behaviors.

In the event that you are struggling with any kind of reoccurring sin, you may want to ask God to take away any pleasure that you have been receiving, and replace it with a horribly sick feeling. A good prayer to begin this process would be, Dear Heavenly Father, I come before you a sinner seeking your mercy and forgiveness. I have been struggling with the sin of _____ for many years. Please take away all the pleasure that I have been receiving and replace it with a horrible sick feeling. Please magnify the destructive consequences of my sin, so that I may turn away from all forms of unrighteousness, and turn to you as my source of fulfillment in life. Amen.

After you have been able to incorporate the spiritual Antabuse prayer in your own life, it would be possible to pray the same prayer for any other person within your sphere of influence. For example, if a mother had an adult child living in her basement, and every night the young man went to the bar to get drunk, instead of praying deliverance prayers in an attempt to bind the demons that were driving his behaviors, a better prayer would be to ask God to take away all the pleasure that the young man was receiving, and replace it with a horribly sick feeling.

If every time the young man went to the bar he felt horribly sick, he would be highly motivated to change his behaviors.

BREAKING SINFUL AGREEMENTS WITH EVIL

Anytime a person commits a sin, that person is saying *no* to God's purpose and plan for his or her life, and *yes* to some kind of worldly or fleshly desire. Because all sin is a direct violation of God's law, it becomes an open door for the devil. Once a sin has been committed, demonic spirits will continue their assault in an attempt to get that person to sin again. If the devil can get a person to sin once, he will use the same temptation to get that person to sin again.

Once a pattern of sin has been established, the devil will drive that person further away from God and deeper into bondage. The only way for a person to break free would be to denounce all sinful thoughts, words and actions in the name, power and authority of Jesus. After all sinful agreements have been broken, the next step would be to make a complete act of contrition.

To make a complete act of contrition, it will be necessary to see your sin the same way that God sees your sin. You will need to love God more than you love your sin. For example, if a young man commits the sin of fornication by having sex with his girlfriend, and then goes to confession, but has no intention of changing his behaviors, he has *not* made a complete act of contrition. What he is actually saying to God is, "I am sorry that your laws are in direct conflict with my behaviors."

Because the man has *not* made a complete act of contrition, he will usually fall back into the same sinful pattern. He will have more sex with his girlfriend, and then he will go back to confession. His lifestyle will consist of sinning and confessing, and then sinning some more and confessing some more, until at which point the young man will grow so weary of going to confession that he will stop going. When this happens, the devil will drive him deeper into bondage and further away from God.

In order for the young man to make a complete act of contrition, he will need to see his sin the same way God sees his sin. He will need to renounce the devil's lies and renew his mind in Christ. In order for this to occur, the young man may need to stop watching worldly movies and television shows where premarital sex is glorified. He will also need the Holy Spirit's help to understand how the sin of fornication is harming his relationship with God, and how it may be harming God's plan for his marriage and future wife.

In order to make a complete act of contrition, it will be helpful to understand why God in his great love for humanity has given us his laws for our well-being and protection. It would also be helpful for the young man to realize how his sin harms other people and what would happen if he got his girlfriend pregnant outside of a God-approved marriage, or what would happen if he contracted a venereal disease, or was infected by the HIV virus and died of AIDS. Once a young man sees his sin the same way God sees his sin, he will be more motivated to change his behaviors and turn back to the Lord's loving guidance and protection.

Another example of making a complete act of contrition comes from a thief who stole his neighbor's bicycle. If the thief were caught on a security video, he would probably say that he was *sorry* for his actions, but if the thief didn't want to return the bicycle, then it would *not* be a complete act of contrition. The thief may be sorry that he was caught, but if he viewed his sin the same way God viewed his sin, then he would want to return the bicycle, because God loves and cares about his neighbor.

It is for this reason that 1 Peter 4:8 says, *Maintain constant love for one another, for love covers a multitude of sins.* If the thief were truly sorry and loved his neighbor, he would have never stolen the bicycle in the first place. If the thief spent less time focusing on his own self-centered and selfish desires, and more time performing loving acts of charity for his neighbors, he would be making a complete act of contrition.

According to the Catechism, contrition is defined as the *sorrow of the soul and detestation for the sin committed, together with the resolution not to sin again. Contrition is the most important act of the penitent, and is necessary for the reception of the Sacrament of Penance.*[1] The Catechism also speaks about our need to repair the harm that our sins have caused other people. For example, we should *return stolen goods, restore the reputation of someone slandered* and *pay compensation for injuries.*[2]

Because all sin is an open door for demonic attack that leads people deeper into bondage, while at the same time hindering our relationship with God and harming God's beloved children, it may be helpful to review the following list of sins along with their corresponding Scripture passages. Once you identify any areas of concern, you may want to spend some time in prayer denouncing the sin of _____ in the name, power and authority of Jesus.

After you break all agreements with evil and ask for the Lord's forgiveness, it will be beneficial to visit the Sacrament of Reconciliation for any venial sins, and necessary to receive the Sacrament of Reconciliation for any mortal sins. After you make a complete act of contrition, it would also be helpful to spend some time performing loving acts of kindness and charity. By doing so, you will be drawing closer to God, while at the same time driving evil out of your life and sphere of influence.

Accepting a bribe	Ex 23:8, Ps 26:9–10
Acting arrogantly	Mk 7:22, Rom 1:30, Jas 4:16
Adultery	Ex 20:14, Mt 19:18, CCC 2380
Astrology	Deut 4:19 & 17:2–5, Acts 7:42–43
Bearing false witness	Ex 20:16, Mt 15:19
Being a hypocrite	Mt 15:7–9
Being consumed by fear	2 Tim 1:7, 1 Jn 4:18
Being angry with others	Mt 5:22, CCC 2302
Being ashamed of Jesus	Mk 8:38, Lk 9:26
Being associated with evil	Rev 18:4–5
Being deceitful	Jer 9:5–6, 2 Cor 11:13, Rom 1:29
Being disobedient toward parents	2 Tim 3:1–2, Rom 1:30
Being hateful	1 Jn 2:9–11, Titus 3:3, CCC 2303
Being prejudiced	Jas 2:1–4 & 9
Bitterness	Acts 8:23, Eph 4:31, Heb 12:15
Breaking an oath	Num 30:2, Deut 23:21–23

Buying or selling spiritual powers	Acts 8:9–24, CCC 2121
Committing an abortion	Ex 21:22, Jer 1:4–5, CCC 2270
Complaining about hardships	Num 11:1, Jude 1:16
Consumed by the love of money	Heb 13:5, 1 Tim 6:9–10, Jas 5:1–3
Coveting your neighbor's property	Ex 20:17, CCC 2539
Cursing and using profanities	Ps 10:7, Rom 3:14, Jas 3:9
Denying Jesus as God's Son	Jn 1:1 & 14, Jn 3:16, 1 Jn 5:10–12
Denying Jesus as the Christ	1 Jn 2:22, 1 Jn 5:10, CCC 161
Denying Jesus before others	Mt 10:33, 1 Jn 2:22
Denying the resurrection of Jesus	Rom 10:9, CCC 14
Despising authority	2 Pet 2:10, Jude 1:8
Despising correction	Heb 12:5
Disobeying God's commandments	1 Jn 2:3–4, CCC 2013
Distorting the meaning of Scripture	2 Pet 3:15–16, Gal 1:6–8, Rev 22:18
Divorce & remarriage (with some exceptions)	Mt 19:9, CCC 2382–2386
Dressing indecently or immodestly	1 Tim 2:9–10, CCC 2522
Dwelling on negative thoughts	Phil 4:4–9
Eating or drinking blood	Lev 3:17, Acts 15:20
Engaging in senseless controversies	Prov 17:14, Titus 3:9, 2 Tim 2:23
Enjoying evil and thinking it's funny	Rom 12:9, Ps 36:4
Ensnared by worldly ways	Mk 4:19, Lk 8:14
Entertaining evil desires	Col 3:5–6
Enticing others to practice witchcraft	Deut 13:6–10, Acts 13:8–12
Failing to accomplish God's will	Mt 7:21–27
Failing to acknowledge guilt	Jer 3:13, CCC 1849–1850
Failing to admit that you're a sinner	1 Jn 1:8–10, CCC 827
Failing to attend church	Heb 10:25, Eccl 4:9–10, CCC 2180
Failing to attend confession	1 Jn 1:9, Jas 5:16, CCC 1457

Failing to do the right thing	Jas 4:17
Failing to give God praise	Eph 5:19–20, Col 3:17
Failing to give God the glory	Lk 17:17–18, Rom 1:21
Failing to honor your father and mother	Ex 20:12, Mt 19:19
Failing to seek first the kingdom of God	2 Chr 7:14, Mt 6:33
Failing to submit and serve the Lord	Lk 19:11–27, Jas 4:13–16, Eph 2:10
Failing to teach God's Word to your children	Deut 6:5–7
Failing to worship God in spirit and truth	Jn 4:24
Filthy conversations	Col 3:8, 1 Peter 2:1
Following desires of the flesh	Rom 8:5–8, Gal 5:16–24, Eph 2:3
Foolish conversations	Mt 12:36, Eph 5:4
Fornication or premarital sex	Mk 7:21, 1 Thess 4:1–8, CCC 2353
Fortune-telling	Deut 18:10–12, Acts 16:16–18
Getting drunk	Prov 20:1, Rom 13:13, 1 Cor 6:10
Getting entangled in worldly ways	2 Tim 2:4, Jas 4:4
Getting involved in senseless controversies	2 Tim 2:23, Titus 3:9
Gluttony and overeating	Prov 23:20–21, Phil 3:19
Gossip and spreading lies	Rom 1:29, 1 Tim 5:13
Greed and selfishness	Lk 12:15, Eph 4:19, Col 3:5–6
Hardness of heart	Heb 3:8 & 15, Eph 4:18
Harming another person's reputation	Ps 101:5, Mk 7:20–23, CCC 2477
Hating your neighbors	Prov 14:21, Lk 18:9
Holding a grudge	Col 3:12–13
Homosexuality	Lev 18:22, Rom 1:24–28, CCC 2357
Husband who does not honor his wife	1 Pet 3:7, Eph 5:25–33
Idolatry	Ezek 16:1–42, 1 Jn 5:21, 1 Cor 10:20
Inviting cult members into your home	2 Jn 1:10–11
Kidnapping	Ex 21:16

Lack of compassion	1 Pet 3:8
Lack of forgiveness	Mt 6:14–15, Mk 11:25–26, Lk 17:4
Lack of love for others	1 Cor 13:1–7
Laziness	Prov 6:6–11, 2 Thess 3:10–13
Letting the sun go down on your anger	Eph 4:26–27, CCC 2302
Living for pleasure	1 Tim 5:6, Jas 5:5, Titus 3:3
Living for worldly and fleshly desires	Rom 8:6–8, Rom 13:14
Loving pleasure more than God	2 Tim 3:4
Loving the ways of the world	1 Jn 2:15–17
Lukewarm for Jesus	Rev 3:15–16
Lust	Mt 5:27–30, Col 3:5–6, CCC 2351
Masturbation	Rom 13:14, Gal 5:16, CCC 2352
Murder	Ex 20:13, Mt 19:18, CCC 2268
Neglecting the poor	Ezek 16:49, Mt 25:31–46
Not being content with what you have	Heb 13:5
Not keeping the Sabbath's day rest	Ex 20:8–11, CCC 2185
Not living by faith	Heb 11:6, Rom 14:22–23, CCC 2087
Not loving God with all your heart	Deut 6:5, Mt 22:37
Not obeying governing laws	Rom 13:1–2, 1 Pet 2:13–14
Not paying taxes	Lk 20:25, Rom 13:6–7
Not producing good fruit	Mt 3:10, Lk 13:6–9
Participating in evil	1 Thess 5:22
Pornography	Mt 5:28, Jas 1:14–15, CCC 2354
Pride	Prov 16:18, Lk 18:9–14, Jas 4:6
Promoting strife	Prov 16:28
Provoking your children to anger	Eph 6:4, CCC 2223
Reading New Age and metaphysical books	Col 2:8
Receiving communion in unworthy manner	1 Cor 11:27–30, CCC 1385

Reciting meaningless prayers to God	Mt 6:7–8, CCC 2608
Refusing to be baptized	Lk 7:30, Jn 3:5, CCC 1257
Refusing to pray for your enemies	Mt 5:43–44, Lk 6:27–28
Refusing to repent	Mt 4:17, Lk 13:3–5, Acts 2:38
Rejecting God's calling	Mt 22:1–14, Acts 7:51
Rejecting the Lord's teachings	Jn 12:48–49
Rejecting the Word of God	1 Sam 15:23, Jer 8:9, CCC 105
Resisting God's discipline	Heb 12:7–8
Resisting the Holy Spirit	Acts 7:51
Seeking after false teachers	Mt 24:24, 2 Tim 4:3–4
Seeking signs and wonders	Mt 16:4, Lk 11:29
Selfish ambitions	Phil 2:21, Jas 3:16
Sex outside of God-approved marriage	1 Cor 6:15–20, Eph 5:3, CCC 2390
Smoking	Rom 13:14, 1 Pet 1:15, CCC 2290
Sowing discord within a family	Prov 6:16 & 19
Speaking bombastic nonsense	2 Pet 2:18
Spreading false information	Ex 23:1, CCC 2477–2485
Stealing	Ex 20:15, Mk 7:21–23, CCC 2408
Swollen with conceit	1 Tim 3:6, 2 Tim 3:2–4
Taking the Lord's name in vain	Ex 20:7
Talking too much	Jas 1:19, 1 Tim 5:13
Tattooing marks on your body	Lev 19:28
Teaching demonic doctrines	1 Tim 1:3–4, 4:1
Telling lies	Jn 8:44, Rev 21:8, CCC 2483
Watching immorality on television	Ps 101:3–4, CCC 1809
Wearing transgender clothing	Deut 22:5
Witchcraft	Deut 18:10–13, Ex 22:18, Gal 5:20
Withholding tithes and offerings from God	Lev 27:30, Mal 3:8–10

Worrying about everything	Phil 4:6
Worshiping angels instead of God	Col 2:18–19, Rev 22:8–9
Worshiping false gods	Ex 20:3, Ps 81:9, CCC 2113
Worshiping graven images	Ex 20:4–6 & 32:7–8, Deut 7:25–26

As an extra credit assignment, try to identify at least three sins that have not been included on this list along with their corresponding Scripture passages.

1. _____

2. _____

3. _____

SEXUAL IMMORALITY & UNHEALTHY SOUL-TIES

One of the most profound teachings that Jesus presented during his Sermon on the Mount comes from Matthew 5:17–19, when the Lord said, *"Do not think that I have come to abolish the law or the prophets; I have come not to abolish but to fulfill. For truly I tell you, until heaven and earth pass away, not one letter, not one stroke of a letter, will pass from the law until all is accomplished.*

"Therefore, whoever breaks one of the least of these commandments, and teaches others to do the same, will be called least in the kingdom of heaven; but whoever does them and teaches them will be called great in the kingdom of heaven."

After making this statement, Jesus continued his teaching by describing several sins, and then he amplified and expanded upon their meanings. For example, in Matthew 5:27–29, Jesus says, *"You have heard that it was said, 'You shall not commit adultery.' But I say to you that everyone who looks at a woman with lust has already committed adultery with her in his heart. If your right eye causes you to sin, tear it out and throw it away; it is better for you to lose one of your members than for your whole body to be thrown into hell."*

After presenting this teaching, there may have been many people in the audience that were wondering why Jesus was being so strict with the laws of sexual morality. At the time, there were many pagan temples surrounding Israel where the worshipers of a Canaanite fertility god named Baal would perform human sexual acts with male and female prostitutes.

Although it was believed that Baal had the ability to make the land, animals and humans fertile, when people worshiped Baal with sexual acts, they were actually making agreements with demonic spirits. Once a demonic spirit gained access to a person's life, it would drive that person deeper into bondage and hinder that person's relationship with God.

A good example of how the devil can hinder a person's relationship with God comes from a young man named Thomas who was having premarital sex with his girlfriend. The devil's assault on Thomas began many years before he met his girlfriend. When Thomas was in grade school, the devil began filling his mind with lies and sexually perverted images that he watched on television. In many of these television shows, sexual acts between unmarried couples and same-sex couples were portrayed as cool, fun and normal.

If the devil can get Thomas to believe that having premarital sex is cool, fun and normal, then after he started having sex with his girlfriend, the devil could use those sins to hinder his relationship with God. Once Thomas has been separated from God's protection and guidance (through the sin of fornication), demonic spirits will drive him deeper into bondage. Because the devil only has one purpose, *to steal and kill and destroy,*[1] demonic spirits will do everything within their power to break Thomas's heart, destroy his finances and interfere with God's purpose and plan for his life.

One way for Thomas to permanently change the direction of his life would be to get his girlfriend pregnant. Once Thomas's sperm fertilizes his girlfriend's egg, at the exact moment of conception, a human life has been created. Once another human life has been created outside of a God-approved marriage, it has the potential to totally change everything. Although Thomas may have started out having sex with his girlfriend because it was cool, fun and normal, he will now be faced with a very difficult and serious decision.

One option for Thomas in this situation would be to marry his girlfriend and have the baby. In the event that it was God's will for this couple to get married, this option could still have serious consequences, because it may *not* be in the Lord's timing for this couple to get married at this point in their lives. For example, maybe Thomas would not be in a place of financial stability to afford all the expenses associated with bringing a child into the world and supporting his future wife.

Another option for this couple would be to get married even though it was *not* God's will. Just because a couple gets married in a church doesn't mean they have God's approval. Thousands of couples walk down the aisle every year without ever asking the Lord's permission. In the event that this couple gets married outside of God's will, their marriage may end in a divorce. Ten years after Thomas marries his girlfriend outside of God's will, he may be forced to pay attorney fees, child support and alimony for a very long time.

Another option the devil will try to promote would be to encourage this young couple to have an abortion. Although this option may seem like the most convenient, killing an unborn baby is a very serious sin. Not only will killing an unborn child provide an open door for demonic oppression, but it can cause long-term and destructive consequences for all the parties involved. A good example of the destruction that abortion causes comes from the testimonies of women who have suffered negative consequences after terminating their pregnancies.

After having an abortion, one woman described her experience by saying, "For eighteen years I suffered over my abortion. I was angry with myself for not being strong enough. I condemned myself as I thought God had. I did not feel that I deserved to be forgiven for what I had done. I wanted to be punished, and since no one punished me severely enough, I punished myself." In another situation, a woman described her experience by saying, "My abortion has left me empty, alone and in despair. It has taken me to a place I almost couldn't come back from. The self-hatred I see every time I look in the mirror has been my constant companion for the last ten years."[2]

According to statistics provided by Project Rachel Ministry, women who have had an abortion in the past have an eighty-one percent higher risk of mental health issues compared to women who have not had an abortion. These women also have thirty-four percent higher anxiety rates, thirty-seven percent higher depression rates, and more frequent suicidal tendencies compared to those who have not had an abortion.[3] Many women also experience intense grief, an inability to forgive themselves, emotional numbness, eating disorders, lower self-esteem, nightmares, sleep disturbances, difficulty with relationships, panic attacks, flashbacks and a discomfort around babies.[4]

When most unmarried couples have an abortion, they usually experience a breakup a few months later. That's because women have been designed by God to love, nurture and protect their children. When a woman is pressured into killing her unborn baby, she will know that something is wrong in the relationship, and she may ask herself a few questions. For example, she may wonder, "Why would my boyfriend, who says he loves me, want me to kill the child that I instinctually want to protect? If my boyfriend truly loved me, why wouldn't he want to get married and raise a child together?"

If the woman starts to question the authenticity of her boyfriend's love, she may begin to realize that he doesn't really love her as much as he says. She may even realize that her boyfriend was just using her for sex because he thought it was cool, fun and normal. If that's the case, there's a good possibility their relationship will end in a painful breakup a few months after they kill their unborn child.

Another option for the young couple in this situation would be to repent of their sins and turn back to God for guidance. Because God has a purpose and plan for everybody's life, it would be important for Thomas and his girlfriend to pray, fast and seek the Lord's guidance before making any kind of marriage decision. If the Lord was calling Thomas to marry his girlfriend, then he should proceed in obedience. If the Lord was *not* calling Thomas to get married, then he would need to break the sexual soul-ties that were created through the sin of fornication, and go through the painful separation process.

In the event that God was *not* calling this couple to get married, and that the Lord wanted the young woman to give her child up for adoption, the devil will do everything within his power to make sure she keeps her baby. That way, the child would grow up with the potential of feeling unloved and unwanted, while being bounced back and forth between his mother's and father's custody. In addition to robbing the child of a normal upbringing, Thomas may also have to pay attorney fees, child support and court costs.

Because God loves Thomas and his girlfriend, he has given us strict laws concerning sexual morality. God designed sex exclusively for marriage, not any kind of civil union, but only for a God-approved marriage between a man and woman. The word in the Bible that describes sex outside of a God-approved marriage is *fornication.*

There are many warnings in the Bible about fornication, including Mark 7:21–23, where Jesus says, *"For it is from within, from the human heart, that evil intentions come: fornication, theft, murder, adultery, avarice, wickedness, deceit, licentiousness, envy, slander, pride, folly. All these evil things come from within, and they defile a person."*

According to the dictionary, the word *fornication* is defined as, "voluntary sexual intercourse between an unmarried man and an unmarried woman."[5] The use of the word *unmarried* is important because if an unmarried man had sex with a married woman (another man's wife), then it would be called *adultery.*

Because God loves and cares about humanity, he has given us laws concerning every kind of sexual sin imaginable. For example, the sin of having sex with animals is called *bestiality,* and it has been condemned in

Leviticus 18:23, when the Lord said, *"You shall not have sexual relations with any animal and defile yourself with it, nor shall any woman give herself to an animal to have sexual relations with it: it is perversion."*

The sin of homosexuality has been condemned in Leviticus 18:22, when the Lord said, *"You shall not lie with a male as with a woman; it is an abomination."* Other Bible verses that condemn homosexuality (along with sodomy) would include Leviticus 20:13, Romans 1:24–28, 1 Corinthians 6:9–10 and 1 Timothy 1:10–11.

The word *licentiousness* means disregarding the laws of sexual morality. This word has been used in Scripture many times, including Mark 7:22, Romans 13:13, Galatians 5:19 and Ephesians 4:19. Because God designed sex between one man and one woman in a God-approved marriage, any kind of sexual activity (thought, word or action) outside of a God-approved marriage would be considered *sexual immorality.*

Even transgender cross-dressing has been condemned in Deuteronomy 22:5, when the Lord said, *"A woman shall not wear a man's apparel, nor shall a man put on a woman's garment; for whoever does such things is abhorrent to the Lord your God."*

Other destructive consequences of having sex outside of a God-approved marriage would include the bondage of unhealthy sexual soul-ties. The term *soul-ties* was first introduced in 1 Samuel 18:1, where *the soul of Jonathan was bound to the soul of David, and Jonathan loved him as his own soul.* Although this may be a description of a healthy soul-tie, it's also possible to form unhealthy soul-ties.

Unhealthy soul-ties are formed when a man has sex with a woman, and after the couple breaks up, the spiritual bonds that have been formed remain intact. Because marriage has been designed to last a lifetime, God designed sex to bond married couples together for the rest of their lives. When a man is sexually bound together with someone other than his God-approved marriage partner, demonic spirits can access those bonds and interfere with his life.

A good example that describes how sexual soul-ties are formed comes from Saint Paul's letter to the Corinthians that says, *"The body is meant not for fornication but for the Lord, and the Lord for the body. Do you not know that your bodies are members of Christ? Should I therefore take the members of Christ and make them members of a prostitute? Never!*

"Do you not know that whoever is united to a prostitute becomes one body with her? For it is said, 'The two shall be one flesh.' But anyone united to the Lord becomes one spirit with him. Shun fornication! Every sin that a person commits is outside the body; but the fornicator sins against the body itself."[6]

In this Scripture passage, Saint Paul is saying that when a man has sex with a prostitute, a spiritual bond is formed where the man and the prostitute become as one flesh. Another way to view this spiritual connection is that the soul of the man is bound together with the soul of the prostitute in a way that is only designed for a God-approved marriage. Unhealthy soul-ties become an open door for demonic oppression because demonic spirits can access those connections and traffic sexual filth back and forth between parties, even after the couple breaks up.

In the event that you have been involved in a sexual relationship outside of a God-approved marriage, there's an unlimited amount of mercy and grace available. For example, when a woman was caught committing the act of adultery, the Pharisees wanted to stone her to death. In John 8:7, Jesus defended the woman by saying, *"Let anyone among you who is without sin be the first to throw a stone at her."*

When the Pharisees heard the Lord's response, *they went away, one by one, beginning with the elders; and Jesus was left alone with the woman standing before him. Jesus straightened up and said to her, "Woman, where are they? Has no one condemned you?" She said, "No one, sir." And Jesus said, "Neither do I condemn you. Go your way, and from now on do not sin again."*[7]

BREAKING UNHEALTHY SEXUAL SOUL-TIES

You can begin the process of breaking unhealthy soul-ties by repenting of all sexual sins, and then making a commitment to never again have sex outside of a God-approved marriage. After you have confessed every kind of sexual sin and have visited the Sacrament of Reconciliation, the next step would be to break all unhealthy soul-ties in the name, power and authority of Jesus.

Before beginning this process, it may be helpful to make a list of all the people you have had sex with in the past. Once you have completed this list, begin your prayer with a serious act of contrition. Ask the Lord to wash you clean, and reaffirm your commitment to never fall back into any kind of compromised situation.

In order to make a complete act of contrition, it will be necessary to see your sin the same way God sees your sin. Once you recognize just how much harm your sins have caused other people, picture the first person on your list, and then lift that person up to God using the following prayer.

Dear Lord Jesus, please forgive me for having sex with _____. In the name, power and authority of Jesus, I break all sexual soul-ties that I have established with _____. If I have taken any part of _____'s heart, I ask you to remove those parts from me, cleanse and purify them, and restore them back to _____.

If I have given any parts of my heart to _____ that I shouldn't have given, I ask you to take all those parts away from _____, cleanse and purify every aspect of my heart, and restore them back to me, so that my heart will be whole and complete.

After you have prayed a blessing over this person's life, ask Jesus to place his cross between you and that person so that nothing evil or demonic can access your life through those severed connections. After you have prayed everything that the Holy Spirit may be directing you to pray, close your prayer by accepting the Lord's love and forgiveness.

In the event that there's more than one person on your list, continue praying through this procedure with the Holy Spirit's guidance for as long as it takes. In the event that you are still holding onto any personal property from one of your ex-lovers, ask the Holy Spirit what you should do with that property. For example, if you are holding onto an engagement ring, maybe the Holy Spirit would want you to give it back.

If it would cause more harm by giving the engagement ring back, maybe the Holy Spirit would want you to sell the ring and use the money to help the poor. In the event that you are holding onto love notes, cards, pictures or presents, you may want to completely remove them from your environment. By doing so, you will be breaking unhealthy soul-ties, and making more room for God's love, healing and forgiveness in your life.

AVOIDING UNHEALTHY RELATIONSHIPS

One of the easiest ways for the devil to attack a person is through unhealthy relationships. It is for this reason that Sacred Scripture warns us not to be mismatched with unbelievers. According to 1 Corinthians 5:11, Saint Paul says, *"I am writing to you not to associate with anyone who bears the name of brother or sister who is sexually immoral or greedy, or is an idolater, reviler, drunkard, or robber. Do not even eat with such a one."*

A good example of how the devil can attack a person through an unhealthy relationship comes from a recovering alcoholic named Jim. After Jim lost his job working at a lumberyard, he was evicted from his apartment because he couldn't pay the rent. Eventually Jim found himself living in a homeless shelter where he hit bottom and made a commitment to stop drinking and getting high on drugs.

Because the devil didn't want to let Jim go without a fight, he commissioned an assignment of demonic spirits to harass him with seductive temptations about how good it would feel to get high just one more time. Because Jim made a commitment to serve the Lord, he was able to stand strong and resist the devil's temptations by taking his negative thoughts captive. Every day Jim would rebuke the devil's lies with a quote from

James 4:7–8, that said, *Resist the devil, and he will flee from you. Draw near to God, and he will draw near to you.*

Because the devil was not able to tempt Jim using the normal methods that had worked in the past, he decided to turn up the heat and bring in one of Jim's old drinking buddies named Ricky. Because the devil had a long history of using Ricky as a puppet to accomplish his will, it was very easy for the demons to influence Ricky's thoughts and motivate him into action. Because Jim hadn't spoken to Ricky in a long time, when the two men met on a street corner one afternoon, Ricky appeared to be very concerned for Jim's well-being.

After Jim told Ricky that he had stopped drinking, Ricky wanted to invite his long-lost friend to his favorite sports bar so they could reminisce about old times. Even though Jim was lonely and wanted to spend time with his friend, he responded by saying, "I'm sorry, but I have been living in a shelter. I need to find a job so that I can get back on my feet."

"Oh, come on!" Ricky said. "Don't be a crybaby."

"I'm really sorry, but not today," Jim said.

"Maybe Freddy the bricklayer could give you a job? He's always looking for help. Let's just go and ask around," Ricky said. "It will be my treat."

Because the demonic spirits were not able to get Jim to visit the sports bar, they decided to change the direction of their attack by prompting Ricky to offer Jim some free drugs as a way to honor their long-lost friendship. Although Jim wanted to take the drugs and get high just one more time, he began to realize what was going on in the spirit realm. Because Ricky had always required payment in advance before giving any-one drugs, he began to wonder why Ricky would want to give him free drugs, especially after telling him about his commitment to serve the Lord.

Because Ricky would never offer free drugs to anyone, Jim started to see the trap that Satan had set to ensnare his soul. As soon as Ricky removed a small plastic bag from his pocket, Jim turned around and walked the other way. He could hear Ricky yelling out after him from a distance saying, "Hey, where are you going? Get back here! Hey, Jesus freak, I'm talking to ya. Get back here, you punk."

In this situation, Jim had a choice to make: Would he part ways with his old drinking buddies so that he could serve the Lord, or would he allow the devil to attack his sobriety through an unhealthy relationship? Because Jim made a decision to leave behind the devil's domain, he also needed to leave behind his worldly and fleshly friends. If Jim failed to distance himself from unhealthy relationships, the devil could use those people to attack his sobriety.

Because Jim remained strong in his commitment to serve the Lord, God began blessing his efforts. Within a short amount of time, Jim was able to find another job working in a warehouse. After saving several paychecks, he was able to rent a small apartment and move out of the shelter. Because Jim continued growing stronger in his relationship with the Lord, a point came in his life where the devil could no longer tempt him to drink or get high on drugs.

If someone offered Jim a thousand dollars to smoke a joint, he would refuse the money because of his love affair with Jesus. When Jim reached a place of spiritual maturity and strength in his walk with the Lord, there came a point in time where Jesus called him back to the homeless shelter to help other drug addicts and alcoholics recover from their addictions.

Another example of how the devil can attack a person through unhealthy relationships comes from a Christian couple who invited a troubled teenager named Wilson to live in their basement. At first, the Christian couple thought they were serving the Lord by offering Wilson a place to live, but then all kinds of strange phenomena started occurring inside their home.

As it turns out, Wilson was involved with witchcraft. When the couple wasn't around, Wilson would perform satanic rituals in their basement by invoking supernatural powers for the purpose of controlling other people, circumstances and events. When Wilson invited demonic spirits into the couple's home, the demons would *not* attack the teenager, because if they did, Wilson would stop practicing witchcraft. Instead, the demons wanted to make Wilson feel powerful and reward his efforts so that he would participate in more rituals.

Once the demonic spirits had been given permission to enter the couple's home through one of their approved guests, they immediately began attacking the couple's marriage. The slightest misunderstanding that would have been normally dismissed would be blown out of proportion and end up turning into a major argument. Along with the hostile atmosphere and increased fighting within the home, the demonic spirits also started inflicting the couple with mysterious forms of illness. Because all these problems started when they invited Wilson into their home, the couple began wondering about the source.

After spending several days in prayer asking if it was really the Lord's will to help the troubled teenager, the Holy Spirit spoke a one-word answer by saying, *witchcraft*. Upon receiving this revelation, the couple confronted Wilson and discovered what he was doing in the basement. Because the couple didn't want to ask Wilson to leave, they had many conversations with him about the dangers of witchcraft, and although Wilson agreed to stop, he continued performing rituals.

Eventually the couple was forced to remove the teenager from their basement. It took several months and ended up being a major battle, but after Wilson vacated the property, the peaceful presence of the Holy Spirit returned to the couple's home. The contentious atmosphere that had contributed to an endless barrage of marital disputes had completely disappeared. After several months had passed, the couple's mysterious forms of illness abated, and their health was restored to normal.

Although the Christian couple had good intentions of helping a troubled teenager, they compromised the spiritual integrity of their home and violated a commandment of Scripture where Saint Paul says, *"Do not be mismatched with unbelievers. For what partnership is there between righteousness and lawlessness? Or what fellowship is there between light and darkness? What agreement does Christ have with Beliar? Or what does a believer share with an unbeliever? What agreement has the temple of God with idols?*

"For we are the temple of the living God; as God said, 'I will live in them and walk among them, and I will be their God, and they shall be my people. Therefore come out from them, and be separate from them, says the Lord, and touch nothing unclean; then I will welcome you, and I will be your father, and you shall be my sons and daughters, says the Lord Almighty.'"[1]

In this passage of Scripture, the term *mismatched* means to be unequally yoked. This term originated from Deuteronomy 22:10, when God said, *"You shall not plow with an ox and a donkey yoked together."* Because a yoke is a wooden frame designed to bind two animals together, it would be cruel to bind a more powerful ox together with a weaker donkey, and then force both animals to accomplish the same task. In order for the donkey to produce the same workload as an ox, a person would need to constantly whip the donkey, which would not only be cruel, but it would place both animals in a very difficult and contentious situation.

In the same way that a yoke would bind an ox and donkey together with a strong bond that would not be easily broken, the Christian couple and teenager were also bound together in a living arrangement that wasn't easily broken. Another characteristic of a yoke is that it limits the freedom of both parties. The ox and donkey would no longer be free to move around as they pleased. In the same way, the spiritual atmosphere of the Christian couple's home was no longer strictly dedicated to Christ. The Christian couple could no longer worship the Lord in spirit and truth while the teenager was worshiping the devil.

Another example of how demonic spirits can attack a person through unhealthy relationships comes from an evangelist named Omar who traveled to Nigeria to minister in the rural villages. Because Omar wanted to set up several outreach locations, he hired three local pastors. By hiring these men, Omar entered into a partnership agreement with them, and in a way, he became yoked together with these men for the duration of the trip.

As soon as Omar arrived in Lagos, he began experiencing problems. Because Omar had spent a lot of time and money traveling to Nigeria to proclaim the Gospel message, he wanted to get right to work. The pastors, on the other hand, were more focused on making money. They didn't want to work in the hot sun all day; instead they wanted to spend time enjoying themselves at Omar's expense inside air-conditioned restaurants.

When Omar asked the pastors if he could visit an outreach location to make sure everything had been set up properly, one of the pastors said, "Everything will be fine. We don't need to go. Just give us more money so that we can pay our driver." When Omar arrived at the village the following day, he discovered that all the men had left early in the morning to work in the fields, and that no one told the village chief about the outreach meeting. When Omar confronted the pastors about the lack of preparation, they made many excuses and gathered a few women together so that he could deliver his message.

Because Omar had placed a yoke around his neck with these pastors, he was limited in his abilities to produce a rich harvest. If Omar had spent more time praying, asking the Lord's permission to work with these men, the Lord could have warned him. In the event that Omar had spent more time seeking the Lord's guidance, he could have searched for better alternatives. If Omar had entered into a partnership with three powerful evangelists, these men could have formed an unstoppable team with enough power to plow the hardest of soil, and in doing so, they could have produced an abundant harvest for the Lord.

Because there are many different types of yokes that we place around our necks on a regular basis, it may be helpful to pray about any kind of personal, business or ministry partnership that you have entered into that may be an open door for demonic attack. In the event that you have entered into an unhealthy personal, business or ministry partnership that is hindering your ability to serve the Lord, you may want to spend some time in prayer asking God to show you how he wants you to proceed.

A simple prayer to begin this process would be, Dear Heavenly Father, I surrender every aspect of my life into your loving hands. I surrender all my hopes, plans and dreams. I offer you my friendships, personal relationships, business partnerships, marriage, family and children. I give you permission to remove any destructive elements, problems or attitudes from my life, heart and environment.

I realize that your Word requires me to separate myself from unhealthy friendships and partnerships. I am very sorry for entering into an unhealthy relationship with _____. Please break all unhealthy soul-ties between _____ and myself. Please place your cross between us, so that the power of your cross can minister to both _____ and myself, for as long as your sovereignty permits.

Please speak to me Lord on how you want me to proceed in all my relationships. If my relationship with _____ is not your divine will for my life, I ask you to close the door and seal it shut with your precious blood. If this relationship is within your will, I ask you to bless and sanctify it in a way that will help me to grow in holiness.

Dear Lord Jesus, I want to accomplish your will in my life. Open my ears so that I may hear your softly spoken voice. Come Holy Spirit, speak to my heart so that I will know your divine will for my life. Please show me how you want me to proceed. May your wisdom, direction and insight be released at this very moment, and may it continue for as long as your sovereignty permits. Amen.

TAKING NEGATIVE THOUGHTS CAPTIVE

When a man named John found himself plagued by reoccurring negative thoughts, he began to wonder about their source. At least once a week, a situation from his past involving police officers would surface in his mind and cause him to experience negative emotions that would rob him of peace and joy. Although these thoughts seemed to come out of nowhere, they had a source, and in an attempt to eliminate them from his life, John began asking the Lord to take him back into his past.

Several years ago when John was at home, he made a long distance call to New York. When dialing the numbers of 1-914, the one button on his phone stuck, and he accidentally dialed 1-911. Because the call didn't seem to go through, John hung up and redialed the correct number. While John was talking to his friend in New York, the emergency operator called him back, and because the line was busy, she sent several police officers to his door to make sure everything was okay.

When John answered the door, the officers assumed a domestic dispute was in progress. They wanted to inspect John's house to make sure that his wife didn't call 911. When John said, "I'm the only one home, and I didn't call 911," one of the officers became belligerent.

He accused John of being a liar and wanted to enter his home.

Because there was a glass security door between John and the officers, he told them, "You don't have the right to search my property without a warrant."

"We have probable cause!" one of the police officers said.

"If you want to search my home, you will need a warrant signed by a judge! Once you have a warrant, you don't need to ask my permission. You can just kick down my door and search my property anytime you want."

After John and the officers exchanged a few more heated words, one of the officers grabbed the door's handle in an attempt to force his way inside. Because the glass security door was locked, John quickly closed the interior door and called 911. The same emergency operator who sent the police to his home in the first place answered the phone, and she sent his call to a supervisor, who also wanted to search his home without a warrant.

Because a large police force was gathering in front of John's home, he allowed one of the officers to inspect his property, providing that the officer removed his shoes. Because John was the only person home, and because there were no guns, drugs or crimes being committed inside the house, the police officer inspected every room of his home and then wanted to see John's driver's license. The officer wanted to run John's name to see if he had a criminal record and to make sure he didn't have any outstanding warrants.

Because John was an upstanding citizen with a clean record and no warrants for his arrest, the officers didn't have any reason to remain on his property, and they eventually left. Although the police officers departed without causing any additional problems, John found himself constantly plagued with negative thoughts regarding the incident. Even though John wanted to stand his ground and make the officers respect his 4th Amendment rights, because a large police force had surrounded his home, he wanted to de-escalate the situation as soon as possible.

One reason why John wanted to de-escalate the situation was that he didn't want his neighbors to look at all the police cars and form a negative perception about his family. John also knew it was unwise to allow police officers inside his home, because if one of the officers found a toy gun in his child's bedroom, the officer could draw his weapon and shoot John. If anyone questioned the shooting, all the officer would need to say was that John pointed a gun at him first.

Another reason why John didn't want to let police officers inside his house was due to a law called *civil asset seizure*. According to this law, if a police officer pulled a man over for a routine traffic stop, and after searching the vehicle, the officer found drugs along with ten thousand dollars in cash, the police would have the right to confiscate the man's money. Under civil asset seizure laws, the police could assume the cash was being used in a crime, and that crime would give them the right to keep the money.

In the same way the police would have the right to confiscate drug money that they assumed had been involved in a crime, they could also confiscate any other type of personal property, including cars, houses or boats. For example, if John had a flat-screen television inside his home, the police could assume the television had been involved in a crime and confiscate it under civil asset seizure laws. Or maybe the police had a bag of drugs in the trunk of their car that they wanted to plant inside John's home so that they could arrest him and teach him a lesson.

Although John had plenty of reasons why he didn't want police officers searching his home without a warrant, it didn't explain why he continued experiencing negative thoughts. Because John wanted to forget about this situation, he tried to control his negative thoughts by using a cognitive form of therapy from Philippians 4:8, which says, *Whatever is true, whatever is honorable, whatever is just, whatever is pure, whatever is pleasing, whatever is commendable, if there is any excellence and if there is anything worthy of praise, think about these things.*

In an attempt to apply this verse to his life, John began thinking more positive thoughts. Whenever a negative thought entered his mind, John would stop himself and meditate on a more positive outcome. For example, John began wondering if he could have avoided a home inspection if he had been more loving and kind to the police officers. Instead of getting into a heated argument about the meaning of *probable cause,* John could have stood firm in his rights, yet at the same time, he could have connected with the officers on a more personal level.

Because John's efforts to take his negative thoughts captive didn't seem to be working, he began to search his heart to see if he had committed some kind of sin.

Although John regretted not looking through the peep-hole before opening the door, he didn't feel that he did anything wrong. Because Ephesians 4:26 says, *Be angry but do not sin; do not let the sun go down on your anger,* John began wondering if he had been withholding forgiveness, or if the lack of forgiveness was allowing the devil to plague his thoughts as a form of harassment.

Because anger is an emotional response to being hurt or threatened, John lifted the situation to the Lord in prayer. During his prayer time, John acknowledged the fact that he felt threatened by the police officers. John also acknowledged that when the officers violated his privacy and accused him of lying, it made him angry. After acknowledging his anger and how his rights had been violated, John offered a full release to the Lord by saying, "I forgive them. I turn this situation over to you. I release it into your hands."

Although John had searched his heart and forgiven the officers to the best of his ability, he continued to be assaulted by negative thoughts that seemed to be growing more frequent as time passed. Instead of thinking more positive thoughts, John began imagining what it would be like to take revenge on the officers. He wanted to call 911 and hang up the phone so that the emergency operator would send more police to his house. This time, instead of submitting to the officer's demand for another home inspection, John wanted to video record the conversation and win the argument regarding his 4th Amendment rights.

Because John's negative thoughts continued growing more intense, he asked God to show him the source of the problem. During his prayer time, John asked the Lord, "Why do I keep thinking about this situation, when all I want to do is let it go and have peace?" The Lord responded with a one-word answer by saying, *distraction*. After thinking about the Lord's response, John realized that if he wanted to let the situation go, the negative thoughts were *not* coming from his own free will. Because the Lord called those thoughts a distraction, it would make sense they were *not* coming from the Holy Spirit. That only left one other possibility, the devil.

For some unknown reason, the devil wanted to harass John with reoccurring negative thoughts about his police encounter for the purpose of causing a distraction. Because the devil wanted to interfere with John's peace of mind, he decided to take an active stance against the devil. Instead of waging a physical battle with the police officers, John decided to wage a spiritual war according to 2 Corinthians 10:3–5, which says, *Indeed, we live as human beings, but we do not wage war according to human standards; for the weapons of our warfare are not merely human, but they have divine power to destroy strongholds. We destroy arguments and every proud obstacle raised up against the knowledge of God, and we take every thought captive to obey Christ.*

Because the devil wanted to pick a fight with John over his encounter with the police, John asked the Lord's permission to visit the police station and pray for the officers. Because the Lord gave John permission, he took a plastic water bottle, and added a small amount of blessed salt. After filling the bottle with water, John drove to the police station and started praying. As John walked around the building, he opened the lid on his water bottle and allowed the holy water to slowly drip out, creating a perimeter around the property.

At first, John's prayers were extremely serious. He asked the Lord to confine the police officer's evil intentions inside the police station so that they would not be unleashed on the general public. After making several trips around the building, John's heart began to soften, and he was able to authentically pray for the officer's salvation. He wanted the officers to be convicted of their sins so that they would repent, turn to the Lord Jesus for healing, and be filled with the Holy Spirit.

Because John had returned the devil's attack with a powerful counterattack, the negative thoughts that he had been experiencing stopped immediately. John was able to convert the remaining anger that still lingered deep within his heart into action. If the devil harassed him with another thought about his police encounter, John would put a small amount of blessed salt in his water bottle, and head back to the police station to pray for the officer's conversion and salvation.

STEPS FOR ELIMINATING NEGATIVE THOUGHTS

1 In the event that you have been experiencing negative thoughts, the first step would be to make a commitment to *take every thought captive to obey Christ.[1]* According to Philippians 4:8, we should be thinking about *whatever is true, whatever is honorable, whatever is just, whatever is pure, whatever is pleasing, whatever is commendable, if there is any excellence and if there is anything worthy of praise, think about these things.* By thinking more loving and positive thoughts, you will be allowing and promoting more loving and positive experiences in your life.

2 The next step would be to search your heart to see if you have committed any kind of sin that would give the devil the right to interfere with your thoughts. Because the lack of forgiveness is a sin, you will need to repent of any wrongdoing, and then after receiving the Lord's forgiveness, you will need to forgive other people in the same way that you want to be forgiven. More information on how to work your way through the forgiveness process can be found in a following chapter entitled, "The Importance of Emotional Healing."

3 After working your way through the forgiveness process, the next step would be to pray about staging a counteroffensive against the devil's harassment. If every time the devil harassed you with negative thoughts, you went out of your way to accomplish something positive, the devil would stop his assault. Although the devil may find another way to attack, you could always counter that attack with the Lord's assistance, and in doing so, you would be growing in holiness, while at the same time, advancing God's kingdom here on earth.

THE REDEMPTIVE VALUE OF SUFFERING

One bright and sunny morning when Jesus was teaching on the Sabbath, a woman who had been crippled for eighteen years entered the synagogue. Although she could still walk, she was bent over and couldn't stand up straight. When Jesus saw her, he called her over and said, *"Woman, you are set free from your ailment." When he laid his hands on her, immediately she stood up straight and began praising God.*[1]

Because the religious leaders were indignant that Jesus healed a woman on the Sabbath, they kept saying to the crowd, *"There are six days on which work ought to be done; come on those days and be cured, and not on the Sabbath day."*[2]

Jesus responded by saying, *"You hypocrites! Does not each of you on the Sabbath untie his ox or his donkey from the manger, and lead it away to give it water? And ought not this woman, a daughter of Abraham whom Satan bound for eighteen long years, be set free from this bondage on the Sabbath day?"*[3]

Although we do not know how demonic spirits gained access to this woman's life, we do know that demons were the root cause of her medical condition. Once the demonic spirits had gained access to her life, they started attacking her body, causing a deformity in her spine. Although this woman had visited many physicians, no one could help her or provide her with any relief.

In a different situation, another woman had been suffering hemorrhages for twelve years. She had visited many doctors, spent all her money, and her condition only grew worse. When she heard that Jesus was visiting the area, she pressed her way through the crowd *and touched his cloak, for she said, "If I but touch his clothes, I will be made well."*[4]

Immediately her hemorrhage stopped; and she felt in her body that she was healed of her disease. Immediately aware that power had gone forth from him, Jesus turned about in the crowd and said, "Who touched my clothes?"[5]

The disciples who were standing nearby said, *"You see the crowd pressing in on you; how can you say, 'Who touched me?'"*

He looked all around to see who had done it. But the woman, knowing what had happened to her, came in fear and trembling, fell down before him, and told him the whole truth.[6]

Jesus reached out his hand, helped the woman to her feet and said, *"Daughter, your faith has made you well; go in peace, and be healed of your disease."*[7]

In both of these situations, it was God's will to provide instant healing to these women. Because God doesn't inflict sickness and disease on people, we know that there are only a few possible sources for all our modern-day medical problems. One source comes from a physical, chemical or biological response to our environment, and the other source comes from the demonic.

When Saint Paul was given a *thorn in the flesh*, he described the experience by saying, *"Therefore, to keep me from being too elated, a thorn was given me in the flesh, a messenger of Satan to torment me, to keep me from being too elated."*[8] Although we don't know what type of thorn Paul was experiencing, we do know that it was *a messenger of Satan.*[9] Some Bible scholars have suggested that Paul's thorn could have been a physical disability, an illness, or even a description for a religious leader who was opposing the Gospel message.

In the event that demonic spirits were causing a person to experience a thorn in the flesh, they will do everything in their power to remain hidden. For example, if the crippled woman discovered that demons had been causing her infirmity, she would have started praying against them. Once the crippled woman discovered how the demonic spirits had gained access to her life, she could have repented of those sins, and sealed the door shut. Once her sinful agreements had been broken, the demons would be forced to leave her life, and she would recover.

One way demonic spirits can remain hidden and unhindered to operate in a person's life is through lies. Because Satan is *a liar and the father of lies,*[10] demonic spirits will whisper lies into the minds and hearts of their victims. One lie the demons could have used on the hemorrhaging woman was that God wanted her to suffer. Deceptive spirits could have said, "God is angry with you, and he has given you a thorn in the flesh."

If the hemorrhaging woman believed that it was God's will for her to bleed, she would have never approached Jesus for healing. If the crippled woman believed that it was God's will for her suffer, demonic spirits could have remained hidden and unhindered to operate in her life. Because God's truth has the power to set people free, Satan will continue disseminating distorted information about our need to suffer in an attempt to hold people in bondage.

One way that Satan holds people in bondage is by disseminating distorted information about the lives of the saints. A good example of a saint who experienced a lot of suffering comes from Saint Bernadette Soubirous of Lourdes. In one example from Saint Bernadette's life, a group of visitors to her convent asked if she knew about all the miraculous healings that were occurring at Lourdes. The visitors wanted to know why Saint Bernadette didn't go to Lourdes to be healed. Saint Bernadette responded to the visitor's question by saying, "You see, my business is to be ill."[11]

The visitors didn't understand Saint Bernadette's response because Saint Bernadette wanted to suffer. Saint Bernadette wanted to suffer because she wanted to offer up her sufferings to make up for the sins of other people. Because Saint Bernadette wanted to suffer, she spent a lot of time in excruciating pain. After spending most of her life in agony, Saint Bernadette died at the age of thirty-five due to a bacterial infection (tuberculosis) affecting the bones in her legs.[12]

Even though it may have been God's will for Saint Bernadette to suffer, according to the Catechism in section 67, a person's *private revelations* do not belong in the *deposit of faith*. When Saint Bernadette received an apparition from Our Lady of Lourdes about the direction of her life, her private revelations would only apply to her own personal situation. If Saint Bernadette was called to a life of suffering, then her private revelations would *not* apply to the rest of the Church, especially if they conflicted with the truth found in Sacred Scripture.

When we study Sacred Scripture, we see that God is a loving Heavenly Father who wants to bless, protect and provide good gifts to his obedient children. We also see in Scripture that the devil is a liar, and only has one purpose, *to steal and kill and destroy.*[13] Throughout the entire Bible, we see Satan causing suffering, sickness and disease. For example, in the Book of Job, *Satan went out from the presence of the Lord, and inflicted loathsome sores on Job from the sole of his foot to the crown of his head.*[14]

In Matthew 17:18, when a young boy had been suffering with epilepsy, *Jesus rebuked the demon, and it came out of him, and the boy was cured instantly.* The Lord's entire ministry was focused on proclaiming liberty to the captives, casting out demons and healing the sick. For example, after Jesus healed Peter's mother-in-law, *they brought to him many who were possessed with demons; and he cast out the spirits with a word, and cured all who were sick. This was to fulfill what had been spoken through the prophet Isaiah, "He took our infirmities and bore our diseases."*[15]

Because the devil has a long history of causing sickness and disease, it would be wise to ask God to show you the source of any prolonged medical problem, especially if you cannot find any doctors who can properly diagnose the situation. A good example of a mysterious medical condition comes from a young lady named Judy who had been experiencing migraine headaches for many years. After reading several Internet articles about the life of Saint Bernadette, Judy began offering up her pain in an attempt to save poor souls from purgatory.

Because Judy's headaches started growing more intense, and began interfering with her ability to focus at work, she started praying about the source of the problem. During her prayer time, Judy found herself conflicted with opposing viewpoints. Did God give her a thorn in the flesh so that she could suffer the same as Saint Bernadette, or did God want to heal her so that her headaches wouldn't interfere with her marriage, family and ministry efforts? Did God want a strong servant to accomplish his will, or did God want a sick, suffering servant who was constantly in pain?

As Judy continued growing in her faith, she started asking the Lord specific questions about her situation. The first question that Judy asked was, "Is it your will that I suffer migraine headaches?" When the Lord answered her question by saying *no*, Judy's next question was, "Are demonic spirits causing my headaches?" Because the Lord answered her question by saying *no*, Judy concluded that the source of her headaches had to be some kind of physiological response to her environment.

If the headaches were *not* coming from God, and if they were *not* coming from the devil, then maybe they were being caused by something in her diet. Or maybe the headaches were an early warning sign of a more serious medical condition such as a brain tumor. Because Sacred Scripture instructed Judy to ask so that the answer would be given, and to search so that she could find, she continued pressing deeper into this issue.

Eventually Judy discovered that her headaches were being caused by an excessive amount of salt in her diet. As soon as Judy eliminated all commercially processed foods from her diet, she was able to reduce her sodium intake, and afterward her headaches completely disappeared. Other possible causes for migraine headaches would include the use of artificial sweeteners that contain neurotoxins, being deficient in omega-3 fatty acids, dehydration and the lack of sleep.

In another example, a man named Kevin was hiking downhill over large rocks. After losing his balance, he slipped and fell to the ground. Immediately a sharp, stabbing pain consumed his right foot. Although Kevin was able to put his shoe back on and continue walking, later that evening the pain became unbearable. As he lay in bed for several hours trying to fall asleep, he began to pray.

At first Kevin asked God to be healed. He wanted the pain to stop so that he could fall asleep and get a good night's rest. Because the pain didn't subside, but appeared to be growing more intense and rising up his leg, Kevin wondered if there was a greater meaning to the painful experience. For example, did God want him to suffer so that he could offer it up and save poor souls from purgatory? Or did God want to inflict him with a thorn in the flesh to teach him some kind of spiritual lesson?

The only way for Kevin to know the answers to these questions was to engage the Lord in an authentic conversation. In the event that God wanted to teach Kevin a lesson, and was using the pain in his foot to get his attention, then it would be wise for Kevin to ask God what he wanted. If God wanted to teach Kevin a lesson, instead of asking for healing, Kevin should be asking, "What are you trying to show me?" If God wanted to use the painful experience to help Kevin grow in holiness, he should be asking, "What changes do you want me to make in my life?"

If Kevin had a history of getting drunk and falling down sets of stairs, then it would make sense that God may be confronting Kevin about his drinking problem. If Kevin had been ignoring the Holy Spirit's warnings, then God in his great love may allow this painful event to occur to get Kevin's attention. If Kevin were getting drunk, then any form of suffering that he may experience would be a direct result of his own sinful actions, but because Kevin is very athletic and didn't consume any alcohol, we can rule out the possibility that the hiking accident occurred because of intoxication.

As Kevin continued lying awake in bed that evening, he decided to change the direction of his prayer. Instead of asking God for healing, he decided to start offering God praise and worship for the painful experience. He said, "Thank you, Jesus! You are the Lord of my life. What changes do you want me to make in my life? If there's anything you want to show me, please open my eyes to see clearly. Please speak to your servant. Open my ears, so that I can hear your voice and be obedient."

Because Kevin wasn't feeling that the Lord wanted him to make any changes regarding the direction of his life, he began praying about the concept of suffering. He started by asking the Lord a simple question, "Do you want me to suffer?" After resting in the Sacred Silence and listening for the Lord's response, Kevin continued asking more questions. Because he didn't hear anything from God, he said, "Are you calling me to suffer, and should I be offering this pain up to you?"

Because Kevin never received any personal revelations from the Lord about his need to suffer, he decided to change the direction of his prayer. Because the pain that he was experiencing was several times greater than what he had experienced after falling on the rocky hillside, he began to wonder about the possibility of demonic influence. If demonic spirits had the ability to increase his pain, then he didn't want to accept anything they were doing, but instead, he wanted to fight against them. In the same way that Jesus ministered to Peter's mother-in-law by rebuking the fever, Kevin started rebuking the pain and commanding anything evil or demonic that may be attacking his body to flee in the name of Jesus.

After praying several spiritual warfare prayers, Kevin rose up out of bed and began to walk. After taking a few steps, he felt a tiny pop in the injured area of his foot, as if one of the small bones had snapped back into its proper joint. Although Kevin's foot was still painful, it felt as if a splinter buried deep in his flesh had just been removed. Immediately Kevin started praising God. He was able to quickly fall asleep that evening, and within a few days, he made a complete recovery.

In the event that you (or one of your friends or family members) has been suffering from some mysterious form of illness that no doctor can properly diagnose, you may want to pray and ask Jesus to show you the source of the problem. One type of suffering comes from our own sin and disobedience. If that's the case, repentance and the Sacrament of Reconciliation will be necessary. Another kind of suffering comes from a God-given thorn in the flesh. For example, in Saint Paul's situation, he was given a thorn in the flesh to keep him from *being too elated.*[16]

In the event that you are receiving so many divine revelations from God, and witnessing so many miraculous healings during your speaking engagements that you cannot keep yourself from being too elated, then one option would be to ask the Lord to remove the thorn. If the Lord responds by saying, *"My grace is sufficient for you, for power is made perfect in weakness,"*[17] then the other option would be to start working on the issue of *being too elated.*[18]

If God is allowing a painful thorn in your flesh for your own spiritual growth, then it would be wise to give God what he wants so that he will remove the thorn. If a painful thorn in the flesh is helping you to grow in holiness, then by working together with God and growing in holiness—giving God what he wants in an attempt to eliminate whatever issue he wants eliminated—then God would be more motivated to remove the thorn, so that you don't have to experience any more pain.

Another kind of suffering comes directly from the devil. Because the devil is very deceptive, he usually gains access to people's lives through the sin of idolatry. Once the sin of idolatry has been committed, the devil will draw that person deeper into bondage. Once a strong hold has been developed, demonic spirits will start attacking that person's health with mysterious forms of illness. In an attempt to remain hidden and undetected, demonic spirits will convince their victims that the source of their problems is coming from God and that God has given them a thorn in the flesh because he wants them to suffer.

The only way to break free from the devil's lies is to turn to God for healing. In the event that you have been suffering a mysterious illness that no doctor can properly diagnose, instead of assuming that God has given you a thorn in the flesh, you may want to get very serious in prayer and ask the Lord to show you the source of the problem.

Because there are only a few possible options for all our modern-day medical problems, including a God-given thorn in the flesh, a demonic attack, or some kind of medical, genetic, chemical or biological response to our environment, it would be helpful to ask Jesus specific questions to narrow down the possibilities. For example, one of the first questions you may want to ask would be, Dear Jesus, do you want me to suffer? Yes or no? Or Dear Jesus, have you given me a thorn in the flesh because you want me to suffer? Yes or no?

If Jesus has *not* given you a thorn in the flesh because he wants you to suffer, then the next question to ask would be, Dear Jesus, is my medical condition coming from a demonic attack? Yes or no? Another question to ask would be, Dear Jesus, have I allowed demonic spirits into my life through some kind of sin? Yes or no? If Jesus says *yes,* then you will need to ask the Holy Spirit to shine the light of truth deep into your heart to discover the open door the devil is using.

If the source of your medical condition is not coming from God or being caused by the devil, that only leaves one other possibility, some kind of medical, physical, chemical or biological response to your environment. If that's the case, you can start asking the Lord specific questions about your health. For example, Dear Jesus, do you want me to make changes to my diet? Yes or no?

If the Lord says *yes,* you can keep asking questions, and then listen for the Lord's response by resting in the Sacred Silence of a contemplative prayer life. After you identify the source of the problem, you can start asking the Lord about the changes he wants you to make. By working in partnership with God through a contemplative prayer life, you should be able to receive all the wisdom, knowledge, understanding, direction and insight that you need to make a complete recovery.

DREAM CHANNELING WITH FALLEN ANGELS

Several years ago a middle-aged woman named Trish began experiencing demonic attacks late at night. Because the attacks were growing more intense, she wanted to meet with a priest. Trish was hoping that a priest could say a few simple prayers to make the devil leave her alone while she was sleeping.

Although Trish couldn't find a priest who was willing to meet with her, she was able to meet with a prayer team that was able to discover the root cause of her problem. During the meeting, Trish described her situation by saying, "Sometimes I can feel them pinning me down at night. I'm still asleep, trying to wake up, but it's like I'm paralyzed and can't move."

"That sounds very unpleasant," one of the prayer team members said. "Maybe we should pray and ask the Holy Spirit to show you the source of the problem."

"Okay," Trish said.

After everybody bowed their heads, one of the prayer ministers asked Jesus to build a canopy of protection around the meeting room. Another member asked the Holy Spirit to show Trish the source of the problem. After several minutes had passed, one of the ministers said, "Why don't you just rest in the Spirit for a moment? We will continue praying for the Lord to show you whatever it is that he wants you to see."

"Very good," Trish said.

After several minutes had passed, one of the prayer team members said, "Tell me what you are sensing."

"I keep getting these dreams at night, and I'm not sure what they mean. Once there was a beautiful lady dressed in blue and white and she was smiling at me. Do you think it could be the Blessed Mother?"

"I'm not sure," the team leader said.

"In another dream, there was a dark room with bars on the windows. I was trapped inside and couldn't get out. What do you think it means?"

"I don't like trying to interpret dreams. It's too difficult to discern what they mean, plus it's way too easy for the devil to interfere with you at night."

"But dreams are so powerful," Trish said. "You can receive wisdom and insight, plus all the biblical examples of how God speaks to people through dreams."

"I like hearing from God when I'm awake," the team leader said. "Many years ago, I asked God to remove all my dreams so that I could fall asleep quickly and I wake up refreshed. I barely remember anything. In fact, that might be a good prayer for you."

"No!" Trish said. "I like my dreams. I don't want to pray that prayer!"

"I'm not asking you to pray anything outside of God's will. If God wants to give you a prophetic dream, then you should be open to receiving it; but if the dreams are coming from the demonic, or just from your subconscious, then let's ask God to completely remove them."

"No, I don't want to pray that prayer!"

Because the atmosphere in the room was growing intense, and Trish was showing signs of resistance, the prayer team decided to take a break.

At this point in the deliverance session, the prayer team discovered that Trish liked having dreams for the purpose of receiving wisdom and insight from the spirit realm (similar to the sin of divination), but at the same time, she wanted to complain about being attacked by the devil at night. When Trish was offered a prayer that would completely remove all her dreams, except for any prophetic messages sent directly from God, she refused and became very defensive.

Although it's true that there are many Old Testament examples that describe how God spoke to his servants through dreams, it's important to understand that the interpretation of those dreams still needed to be verified through prayer during the day. A good example of an Old Testament dream and the correct way to receive its interpretation comes from the Book of Daniel. After Daniel and his companions refused to consume food from the king's table, they were given vegetables to eat and water to drink.

Because these men would rather draw closer to God through prayer and fasting than indulge themselves with rich foods, *the guard continued to withdraw their royal rations and the wine they were to drink, and gave them vegetables. To these four young men God gave knowledge and skill in every aspect of literature and wisdom; Daniel also had insight into all visions and dreams.*[1]

After Daniel and his companions had been promoted to a place of honor within the government, King Nebuchadnezzar received a prophetic dream from the Lord. Because the dream troubled his spirit so much that he could not sleep, he summoned the magicians, enchanters and sorcerers. *When they came in and stood before the king, he said to them, "I have had such a dream that my spirit is troubled by the desire to understand it."*[2]

The men said to the king, *"O king, live forever! Tell your servants the dream, and we will reveal the interpretation."*[3]

The king answered, *"This is a public decree: if you do not tell me both the dream and its interpretation, you shall be torn limb from limb, and your houses shall be laid in ruins. But if you do tell me the dream and its interpretation, you shall receive from me gifts and rewards and great honor. Therefore tell me the dream and its interpretation."*[4]

"Let the king first tell his servants the dream, then we can give its interpretation."[5]

The king answered, *"I know with certainty that you are trying to gain time, because you see I have firmly decreed: if you do not tell me the dream, there is but one verdict for you. You have agreed to speak lying and misleading words to me until things take a turn. Therefore, tell me the dream, and I shall know that you can give me its interpretation."*[6]

"There is no one on earth who can reveal what the king demands! In fact no king, however great and powerful, has ever asked such a thing of any magician or enchanter or Chaldean. The thing that the king is asking

is too difficult, and no one can reveal it to the king except the gods, whose dwelling is not with mortals."[7]

It would have been very easy for the magicians, enchanters and sorcerers to make up any interpretation they wanted, if they knew the king's dream, but because the dream had come from God, no one could provide any detail except for the king and God. If the dream had come from demonic sources, the devil could have imparted the same information to the magicians, enchanters and sorcerers, but because no one could provide any details, the king dispatched the executioners.

When the chief executioner came looking for Daniel, he responded by saying, *"Why is the decree of the king so urgent?"*[8] Because the executioner could not answer, *Daniel went in and requested that the king give him time and he would tell the king the interpretation.*[9]

Then Daniel went to his home and informed his companions, Hananiah, Mishael, and Azariah, and told them to seek mercy from the God of heaven concerning this mystery, so that Daniel and his companions with the rest of the wise men of Babylon might not perish. Then the mystery was revealed to Daniel in a vision of the night, and Daniel blessed the God of heaven.[10]

Although it's true that there are many Old Testament examples describing how God spoke to his servants through dreams at night, in the New Testament, God spoke to his Spirit-filled servants in visions during the day. For example, after Ananias had received the gift of the Holy Spirit, *The Lord said to him in a vision, "Ananias." He answered, "Here I am, Lord." The Lord said to him, "Get up and go to the street called Straight, and at the house of Judas look for a man of Tarsus named Saul."*[11]

In another example, the Lord spoke to Peter in a trance when he *went up on the roof to pray.*[12] In Acts 16:9–10, when God spoke to Saint Paul in a vision at night, the next morning he still needed to pray to make sure the message was coming from God. In order for Paul to receive the correct interpretation about the vision, he needed to maintain an authentic relationship with Jesus and spend time communing with the Lord in prayer during the day, asking questions and discerning the Lord's response.

In Trish's situation, there were only three possible sources for her dreams—her own subconscious, the Holy Spirit or a demonic spirit. If Trish experienced a dream about a bright-red barn, the most logical explanation for this dream would be Trish's own subconscious. Maybe her subconscious captured an image of a red building on television that day, and the dream had no other meaning (or purpose) than her subconscious processing and purging that information.

Another possibility for the dream could be a prophetic message from God. If the Holy Spirit wanted to speak to Trish about a bright-red barn, she would still need to take the image to God in prayer and ask God about the meaning, and more importantly, ask God what he wanted her to do about the bright-red barn. The other possible source for the dream could be the demonic. If demonic spirits had access to Trish's life (through the sin of divination), they could very easily influence her dreams.

The issue that Trish needed to address was if she was using her dreams as a form of divination. Did Trish like having dreams because they provided her with insight into the future? Or did Trish think her dreams were coming from God and that it was her job to interpret the meanings using her own psychic abilities?

In the event that Trish had unknowingly committing the sin of divination with her dream interpretations, then demonic spirits would have the right to attack her at night. If this were the case, Trish would be saying to the spirit realm, "Please speak to me at night and give me dreams that will help me gain wisdom and insight." Then after committing the sin of divination by wanting to communicate with the spirit realm through her dreams, Trish wanted to complain about being attacked by demonic spirits while sleeping.

After taking a break in the prayer session for a few minutes, the prayer team was able to reassemble with Trish. After spending an hour explaining how the sin of divination works, Trish was finally ready to say a simple prayer asking God to remove all her dreams, along with the memory of any dreams that occurred during the night that were *not* directly inspired by God.

In the event that the Holy Spirit wanted to give Trish a prophetic dream about a bright-red barn, then after receiving the dream, Trish could take that image to God in prayer the next day to see what God wanted to say. In the event that Trish continued growing deeper in her Christian walk with the Lord, she should be able to practice contemplative prayer as defined in the Catechism under sections 2709–2719. By practicing contemplative prayer, Trish should be able to ask the Lord specific questions about her life, and after resting in the Sacred Silence and meditating on the Lord's will, she should be able to discern the Lord's answers.

In the event that you have been experiencing demonic attacks during the night, you may want to pray the same prayer that Trish prayed. It's a simple prayer where you ask God to completely remove all dreams except for any dreams that are coming from the Blessed Trinity. There should be a zero-tolerance policy concerning any spiritual entity's ability to interfere with you while you are sleeping. This means that you should *not* be open to receiving any messages from the spirit realm, spirit guides or from spirits of the dead.

A good prayer to begin this process would be, **Dear Heavenly Father, I am very sorry for using my dreams as a source of divination. I denounce all forms of divination, including the interpretation of my dreams, in the name, power and authority of Jesus.**

I cancel all agreements that I have made with demonic spirits of dream interpretation, and I command all demonic spirts that have access to my life through the sin of divination into the abyss to never again return.

Through the mercy and grace of my Lord and Savior, Jesus Christ, I call forth the heavenly host, the holy angels of God, to surround and protect, and cleanse with God's holy light all areas vacated by the forces of evil.

Dear Lord Jesus, please remove all dreams from me, except for any dreams that are coming directly from you. Please send forth your protective angels to stand guard over me as I sleep. Please purify my subconscious during the night with the purity of your infinite love. Amen.

RECEIVING DEMONIC IMPARTATIONS

Another doorway the devil uses to access people's lives occurs through demonic impartations. Because most people would never accept a demonic impartation if they knew what was happening, the devil would need to disguise his true intentions and trick people into thinking they were receiving a blessing.

A good example of how the devil can trick a person into receiving a demonic impartation comes from a woman named Sharon who visited a Reiki practitioner. Although Sharon attended a Catholic grade school and received all the Sacraments, she began exploring different forms of spirituality to see what other religions had to offer. When Sharon read several positive reviews posted on a Reiki website, she decided to give it a try in an attempt to eliminate her lower back pain.

During the session, the Reiki Master asked Sharon to lie down on a medical examination table, and after calling upon the names of his gods, he began to draw Reiki power symbols on Sharon's body using the palm of his hands. The main symbol the Reiki Master used resembled a musical note with a spiral design at the center. When using the power symbol, along with another symbol that resembled a lightening bolt, the practitioner imparted spiritual power into Sharon's body in an attempt to bring healing to her lower back.

When Sharon accepted the Reiki Master's spiritual powers that were directly imparted into her body through the laying on of hands, she was making agreements with demonic spirits. Once the demonic spirits entered Sharon's body, they immediately brought a sense of comfort and relief. The demonic spirits even had the ability to eliminate some of Sharon's back pain. Because Sharon was feeling a little better, she set up several more appointments to see what other services the Reiki Master could provide.

Because the Reiki Master also offered *transcendental meditation,* a Hindu prayer technique where a person chants the names of demonic entities as a mantra; *acupuncture,* a therapy that uses needles to penetrate the skin so that *life energy* can flow through a person's body; *acupressure,* a practice similar to acupuncture except without the needles; *energy medicine, chakra balancing* and *yoga classes,* Sharon eventually found herself swept away by the New Age movement.

Although it may be very easy to see how demonic spirits can access a person's life through New Age techniques and other occult-like practices, what some people fail to understand is that the devil can also use popular television evangelists or miracle faith healers to impart demonic spirits through the laying on of hands.

When a charismatic minister lays his hands on a person with the intention of baptizing that person in the spirit, the spiritual powers that are being imparted may be coming from the Holy Spirit, or they may be coming from demonic spirits. A good example of an authentic impartation of the Holy Spirit comes from the Acts of the Apostles when Peter and John visited Samaria. According to Acts 8:14–21, *When the apostles at Jerusalem heard that Samaria had accepted the word of God, they sent Peter and John to them. The two went down and prayed for them that they might receive the Holy Spirit (for as yet the Spirit had not come upon any of them; they had only been baptized in the name of the Lord Jesus).*

Then Peter and John laid their hands on them, and they received the Holy Spirit. Now when Simon saw that the Spirit was given through the laying on of the apostles' hands, he offered them money, saying, "Give me also this power so that anyone on whom I lay my hands may receive the Holy Spirit."

But Peter said to him, "May your silver perish with you, because you thought you could obtain God's gift with money! You have no part or share in this, for your heart is not right before God."

In this situation, Peter and John were able to impart the Holy Spirit through the laying on of hands. We also see that Simon the magician was so desperate to acquire this ability that he wanted to pay the Apostles a large sum of money. Because an authentic manifestation of the Holy Spirit comes directly from God, for the purpose of helping people accomplish God's will in their lives, it would *not* be possible to pay God any amount of money to obtain this gift. The only way Simon could receive the gift of the Holy Spirit would be to submit his life to the Lord.

If Simon wanted to submit his life to the Lord, the Holy Spirit would have come into his life to provide him with the gifts that he needed to serve God. For example, if God were calling Simon to the healing ministry, as soon as he started visiting the sick and spending time with the hurting, then God's love would flow through him and into the lives of others. As this occurred, the Holy Spirit would provide Simon with the spiritual strength and gifts that he needed to accomplish God's will in his life.

Because Simon was *not* interested in surrendering his life to the Lord, and because he didn't want to serve God in ministry, he would never receive an authentic impartation of the Holy Spirit. The other option for Simon to receive the ability to impart spiritual powers would be for him to make an agreement with the devil. For example, if Simon started chanting the names of demonic entities, or went to a pagan temple and committed the sin of idolatry, then he would be making agreements with demonic spirits.

Once Simon entered into an agreement with demonic spirits through the sin of idolatry, all he would need to do is start conducting healing services. If Simon were able to convince a group of people that he was able to impart spiritual powers, he could have gathered a group of desperate people together. If the people who attended Simon's so-called healing services were open to receiving whatever spiritual powers that he offered, then the demonic spirits that Simon had allowed into his life would have the ability to enter into the lives of those who received his impartations.

In the same way that it would have been possible for Simon to receive spiritual powers that could be transferred to others, it would also be possible for any other modern-day charismatic leader to acquire the same ability. A good example of how this would work comes from a man named Carlos. When Carlos was growing up in Colombia, his entire family was involved in witchcraft. Carlos participated in occult-like activities for most of his life. He continued worshiping Satan until the day one of his friends suggested that he make a pilgrimage to a popular apparition site.

During his visit to the apparition site, Carlos had a mystical encounter with an angel of light. After his spiritual encounter, Carlos didn't denounce any of the sinful agreements that he made with Satan; he simply converted everything that Satan had taught him over the years into a Catholic version of a healing retreat. Carlos was so excited about imparting his new-found spiritual powers that he went directly from witchcraft into a lay apostolate that operated the same as witchcraft.

In an effort to impart his spiritual powers to others, Carlos started renting overnight retreat facilities. After securing a location, he would find a priest who was willing to say Mass for the participants. Because Carlos was able to find a priest for the Masses, it made his events look more official, as if he had ecclesiastical approval for everything that would transpire. Even though Carlos's healing retreats looked very official, many of the participants found themselves a little uncomfortable with some of the occult-like practices.

One reason the retreat participants found themselves uncomfortable comes from a practice called *slaying people in the spirit*. In this exercise, the retreat participants would form a long line, standing side-by-side, while facing the altar. The people who participated in this exercise were encouraged to open their hearts and souls for a special anointing of spiritual power that would *only* come from Carlos or one of his ministers. As Carlos moved down the line of people, he would lay his hands upon the participants' heads and pray a special anointing over them so that they would receive spiritual powers. As the spiritual powers entered the participant's bodies, many people would fall over backward into the arms of catchers who would gently lay them on the ground.

Once on the ground, the participants would generally experience three different types of responses. Although the first group only experienced a brief absentee of mind, they would immediately recover and stand up. Many in this group had no desire to fall over, and they had either submitted to peer pressure or felt pushed over by Carlos. Other participants would fall over and lay on the ground for around ten minutes. During this time, they would fade away in a light trance while still being able to hear the sounds around them.

The third group would fall over backward and remain on the ground for up to six hours. During this time, these people were not conscious of anything. Many people in this group would contribute a significant amount of importance to the amount of time they spent on the ground, because it was during this time that God supposedly conducted his inner-healing work.

According to the people in this group, God's inner healing work was accomplished without any acknowledgement of sin, without the need for repentance, without any need to embrace hurtful past events and without any need to grant forgiveness. Apparently all the healing work occurred automatically on God's operating table by bypassing that person's free will.

Another reason the retreat participants found themselves a little uncomfortable during the slaying in the spirit exercise was all the bizarre noises and behavior that occurred. Some of the participants would experience physical shaking and electric-like surges, while others experienced the loss of strength, fluttering eyelids and uncontrollable laughter. It was even possible for the retreat attendees to experience the feelings of drunkenness, or to see mystical visions and hear audible voices from the spirit realm.

Another concern for many of the retreat attendees was a question about why God would want his beloved children to fall over backward and lay on the ground as a form of worship. In Scripture, we see the devil throwing people to the ground, while Jesus is constantly raising people up.

A good example of how Jesus raises people up comes from the Gospel of Matthew. When Jesus was transfigured before his disciples, *his face shone like the sun, and his clothes became dazzling white. While he was still speaking, suddenly a bright cloud overshadowed them, and from the cloud a voice said, "This is my Son, the Beloved; with him I am well pleased; listen to him!" When the disciples heard this, they fell to the ground and were overcome by fear.*[1]

In this situation, the disciples would have fallen forward as a form of worship with their faces to the ground; they would *not* have fallen over backward while still looking up at the sky. Because Jesus didn't want his disciples to be afraid of God's presence, he immediately *came and touched them, saying, "Get up and do not be afraid."*[2]

Jesus could have left the disciples on the ground for several hours, but instead he wanted his disciples to rise to their feet. Jesus didn't want his disciples to be afraid of God, or to roll around on the ground and make strange noises. He wanted his disciples to be very comfortable with the presence of God, so that they could work in partnership with the Holy Spirit. Jesus wanted the disciples to operate under the power of the Holy Spirit at all times, not fall over backward pretending to be dead every time they experienced God's presence.

Although the Bible offers many other examples where God's servants were called to stand on their feet when encountering the presence of the Lord (Ezekiel 2:1–2, Ezekiel 3:23–24, Daniel 8:17–18), it does not explain why the retreat attendees would act so strangely in the presence of the Holy Spirit, unless of course, the Holy Spirit was never actually present. If that were the case, then the strange behaviors could only be explained by the fact that Carlos had never fully repented of his witchcraft sins, and that he had been imparting demonic spirits to the retreat attendees.

In the event that you have been slain in the spirit, you may want to ask yourself a few questions to examine the motives of your heart. The first question you may want to ask: Why would you want to receive a spiritual impartation from a conference leader, when you could receive an authentic gift directly from God? If God wanted to give you a spiritual gift so that you could serve him in ministry, then why wouldn't God be able to give you that gift in a way where he would receive all the glory?

A good example of how the gifts of the Holy Spirit are imparted comes from the life of Peter. In Acts 2:2–4, Peter received the gift of the Holy Spirit on the day of Pentecost. When all the disciples were gathered together in one place, *suddenly from heaven there came a sound like the rush of a violent wind, and it filled the entire house where they were sitting. Divided tongues, as of fire, appeared among them, and a tongue rested on each of them. All of them were filled with the Holy Spirit and began to speak in other languages, as the Spirit gave them ability.*

After Peter had received the gift of the Holy Spirit, he went forth to work in partnership with God to accomplish the Lord's will in his life. When Peter was visiting the temple late one afternoon, he encountered a lame man who was expecting to receive a few copper coins. *Peter looked intently at him, as did John, and said, "Look at us." And he fixed his attention on them, expecting to receive something from them.*

But Peter said, "I have no silver or gold, but what I have I give you; in the name of Jesus Christ of Nazareth, stand up and walk." And he took him by the right hand and raised him up; and immediately his feet and ankles were made strong. Jumping up, he stood and began to walk, and he entered the temple with them, walking and leaping and praising God.[3]

Because Peter and John had created such a commotion, the temple guards along with the Sadducees and Pharisees had them arrested. The next day, Peter needed more spiritual strength to address the religious leaders, so the power of the Holy Spirit was once again made available to him. According to Acts 4:8–10, *Peter, filled with the Holy Spirit, said to them, "Rulers of the people and elders, if we are questioned today because of a good deed done to someone who was sick and are asked how this man has been healed, let it be known to all of you, and to all the people of Israel, that this man is standing before you in good health by the name of Jesus Christ of Nazareth, whom you crucified, whom God raised from the dead."*

Even though this is the second time Scripture mentions the fact that Peter was *filled with the Holy Spirit,*[4] it was *not* a new kind of spirit. The same Holy Spirit that Peter received on the day of Pentecost was still alive and active in his life. Whenever Peter encountered a difficult ministry situation, the Holy Spirit would provide him with all the spiritual power that he needed to accomplish God's will.

In the same way that Peter was filled with the Holy Spirit on the day of Pentecost, so too, do all Catholics receive the same spiritual power during their Baptism and Confirmation. According to the Catechism in section 1302, *It is evident from its celebration that the effect of the sacrament of Confirmation is the special outpouring of the Holy Spirit as once granted to the apostles on the day of Pentecost.*

Because all baptized and confirmed Catholics have already received the gifts of the Holy Spirit, there wouldn't be any need for anyone to be slain in the spirit, especially when it's not easy to discern what kind of spirit is being imparted. In the event that a man or woman wanted to move with more power of the Holy Spirit, all that person would need to do is surrender his or her life to the Lord and start serving God in the mission field. For example, if God were calling a man to serve him in the healing ministry, then all he would need to do is start visiting the sick and praying for people with love in his heart.

If the man had an authentic calling to minister to those who were sick, then the Holy Spirit would work in partnership with him to accomplish God's will in his life. There wouldn't be any need for that man to receive any other kind of spiritual impartation, because if the conference leaders were operating with the real Holy Spirit, the man would *not* receive anything extra. If the ministers were imparting the real Holy Spirit, and if the real Holy Spirit was already present in the man's life, then nothing would happen, except of course, the man might offend the Lord by seeking spiritual powers from humans, rather than turning to God for all his needs.

If the conference leaders were offering a new or improved kind of spiritual impartation, different from the one the man received during his Baptism and Confirmation, then there's a good chance the man wouldn't want to receive it. That's because there's only one Holy Spirit. You either have the real Holy Spirit alive and active in your life or you don't. If the people at the charismatic conferences are rolling around on the floor, barking like dogs and howling like monkeys, there's a good chance the conference leaders have been imparting demonic spirits.

In the event that you have attended a charismatic conference for the purpose of being slain in the spirit or have received any kind of New Age, occult or satanic impartation, including Reiki or hypnosis, you may want to spend some time in prayer right now to denounce those impartations.

A good prayer to begin this process would be, Dear Heavenly Father, I come before you sinful, in desperate need of your assistance. Please forgive me for all the times I have sought after spiritual impartations that were not your divine will for my life.

In the name of your only begotten Son, Jesus Christ, I denounce all forms of demonic impartations, being slain in the spirit, falling over backward and rolling around on the ground, along with all other demonic impartations, including Reiki and hypnosis. I renounce and forsake my involvement in all of them, and in the name of Jesus Christ who came in the flesh, and by the power of his cross, his blood and his resurrection, I break their hold over my life.

I confess all these sins before you and ask you to cleanse and forgive me. I ask you Lord Jesus to enter my heart and create in me the kind of person you have intended me to be. I ask you to send forth the gifts of your Holy Spirit to baptize me, just as you baptized your disciples on the day of Pentecost. I thank you Heavenly Father for strengthening my inner spirit with the power of your Holy Spirit, so that Christ may dwell in my heart. Amen.

VOWS & SPIRITUALLY BINDING AGREEMENTS

There are many examples of vows in the Old Testament. Some of these spiritually binding agreements served a beneficial purpose, while others provided an open door for the demonic. A good example of a devastating vow comes from the life of a warrior named Jephthah.

When the Ammonite army attacked a small town in Israel, the elders of Gilead asked Jephthah to serve as their commander. Before leading a counteroffensive against the Ammonite army, Jephthah made a vow to the Lord by saying, *"If you will give the Ammonites into my hand, then whoever comes out of the doors of my house to meet me, when I return victorious from the Ammonites, shall be the Lord's, to be offered up by me as a burnt offering."*[1]

When Jephthah returned home after winning the battle, his daughter ran out to greet him. She came out of the house *with timbrels and with dancing. She was his only child; he had no son or daughter except her. When he saw her, he tore his clothes, and said, "Alas, my daughter! You have brought me very low; you have become the cause of great trouble to me. For I have opened my mouth to the Lord, and I cannot take back my vow."*

She said to him, "My father, if you have opened your mouth to the Lord, do to me according to what has gone out of your mouth, now that the Lord has given you vengeance against your enemies, the Ammonites." And she said to her father, "Let this thing be done for me: Grant me two months, so that I may go and wander on the mountains, and bewail my virginity, my companions and I."[2]

At the end of two months, she returned to her father, who did with her according to the vow he had made.[3]

In this situation, the devil was able to use the words of a vow to bring destruction upon Jephthah and his family. Although Jephthah was a warrior that the Lord used to fight against the Ammonites, it was apparent by his actions that he didn't spend a lot of time in prayer before making this vow. Instead of turning to God for direction and insight, he tried to make a deal with God by saying, "If you give me victory in battle, I will give you a sacrifice in exchange."

If Jephthah had maintained a deeper prayer life with the Lord, a vow wouldn't be necessary, because if God was calling Jephthah to fight the Ammonites, then God would have a plan for Jephthah's success. If God had a plan for Jephthah's success, then all he needed to do was ask God to show him the best battle strategy. Jephthah could have worked in partnership with God, and by maintaining a serious prayer life, he would have received all the direction and insight that he needed. But instead of working in partnership with God, Jephthah tried to make a deal with God.

Another example of a vow comes from the life of Jacob. After God appeared to Jacob in a dream, he spoke to him saying, *"Know that I am with you and will keep you wherever you go, and will bring you back to this land; for I will not leave you until I have done what I have promised you."*

Then Jacob woke from his sleep and said, "Surely the Lord is in this place—and I did not know it!" And he was afraid, and said, "How awesome is this place! This is none other than the house of God, and this is the gate of heaven."[4]

Then Jacob made a vow, saying, "If God will be with me, and will keep me in this way that I go, and will give me bread to eat and clothing to wear, so that I come again to my father's house in peace, then the Lord shall be my God, and this stone, which I have set up for a pillar, shall be God's house; and of all that you give me I will surely give one tenth to you."[5]

Because this was Jacob's first encounter with God, he needed a little time to develop an authentic relationship with the Lord. Because there were many false gods that Jacob could have worshiped, he needed time and some real-life experiences to see if God could be trusted. Because God had promised to protect Jacob on his journey, he could have proceeded in faith, trusting God to keep his promise. But because his relationship was in the beginning stages, Jacob wanted to reconfirm his side of the agreement by making a vow.

The same concept of making vows to God also applies to many situations today. Although many people know that God is real, very few people spend time developing an authentic relationship with him. When a tragic event strikes a person's life, many people will turn to God in prayer asking for help. If they don't receive immediate results, they assume that God is not listening, and in their desperation, they will try to make a deal with God in exchange for something they want.

For example, when a young priest named Reverend Martin heard the news that one of his childhood friends had accepted a gay lifestyle, he was deeply distressed. He immediately started praying for a miracle. Because Reverend Martin didn't see immediate results, he made a vow to God offering his most valuable possession (his own life) in exchange for his friend's life. The intention of Reverend Martin's vow was for God to take his life, and in exchange for his death, that God would deliver his friend from a homosexual lifestyle.

These kinds of vows are extremely dangerous because it's very easy for demonic spirits to use the words of this vow against the priest and cause a great deal of destruction. For example, in a similar situation, another priest made the same kind of vow offering his life to God in exchange for his friend's life, and although the priest suffered a tragic death shortly after making the vow, his friend continued living a long life of depravity.

The underlying problem in offering vows to God in exchange for something that you want is that God doesn't need anything, and he already wants to provide abundant blessings to all of his obedient children. In Reverend Martin's situation, God already wanted to deliver the homosexual man from a lifestyle of depravity, and there wasn't any reason for this priest to offer his life, soul or death in exchange for a miracle.

A better prayer for priests in these kinds of situations would be a vow of complete surrender and obedience to the Lord. By surrendering the situation to God, Reverend Martin would be acknowledging

God's lordship over his own life and over his friend's life. God loves Reverend Martin just as much as he loves the homosexual man. God has a purpose and plan for Reverend Martin's life, just like he has a purpose and plan for the homosexual man's life.

By surrendering the situation to God, Reverend Martin would be opening up a spiritual conduit for God to start working. The next step for Reverend Martin in this situation would be obedience. Reverend Martin could have asked God how he wanted him to proceed. Maybe God wanted Reverend Martin to be personally involved with the homosexual man's deliverance process, or maybe God had a different plan. Maybe God wanted to use another priest to speak truth into his friend's life, and after praying against the demonic spirits that were influencing the homosexual man's behaviors, he would have been set free.

SELF-HARMING VOWS

Another device the devil can use to cause destruction in a person's life comes from self-harming vows. For example, if a man becomes so depressed that he doesn't want to live anymore, the demonic spirits that have been assigned to his life can plague his mind and heart with thoughts of suicide. If the demonic entities can get the man to agree with these destructive thoughts, the man would be making agreements with demonic spirits of death.

Once an agreement has been made, the demons will look for an opportunity to bring about the man's desires. For example, if a drunk driver wanted to make a left turn, and the man who didn't want to live anymore was approaching the intersection, the demons could obstruct the drunk driver's vision, causing him to think that it was safe to turn.

Because God loves both the drunk driver and the man with suicidal thoughts, he would want to intervene in this situation to prevent a devastating accident, but because the demonic entities would be operating within their rights, God may allow the accident to occur. The demonic entities would have the right to obscure the drunk driver's vision, because deep in that man's heart, he wanted to zone out and escape reality.

Because the drunk driver didn't want to feel, experience or acknowledge reality, the demons would be giving that man exactly what he wanted. In the same way, the demonic spirits would be giving the man with suicidal thoughts exactly what he wanted. From the demon's perspective, this would be the perfect match. One man wanted to escape reality, while another man wanted to die, so why not bring them together?

CONSECRATION VOWS

Another spiritually binding agreement that can be an open door for demonic oppression is consecration vows. Because some consecration vows promise salvation, while others offer protection from end-time chastisements, it would be helpful to study the words of these vows to see if they contain anything the devil can use to bring destruction into a person's life. Because one of the most popular consecration vows comes from Saint Louis de Montfort, it may be helpful to study the words of this vow as follows.

In the second paragraph of the Saint Louis de Montfort consecration vow the text says, *"But, alas!*

ungrateful and faithless as I have been, I have not kept the promises which I made so solemnly to Thee in my Baptism; I have not fulfilled my obligations; I do not deserve to be called Thy son, nor yet Thy slave; and as there is nothing in me which does not merit Thine anger and Thy repulse, I dare no more come by myself before Thy Most Holy and August Majesty."[6]

One positive aspect about this vow is that the person declaring these words would be acknowledging that they are sinful. According to the Catechism in section 827, *All members of the Church, including her ministers, must acknowledge that they are sinners.*[7] Although some Catholics may feel that there is nothing in them that does not merit the Lord's *anger and repulse,* these feelings would not justify any kind of spiritual shortcut or an alternative form of salvation.

For example, if a man were struggling with a pornography addiction to the point where he hated his life and felt that there was nothing in him that did not merit the Lord's *anger and repulse,* the proper response to his sinful actions would be the Sacrament of Reconciliation on a regular basis. Because the man who is addicted to pornography will need the Lord's help to break free from the demonic spirits that were influencing his behaviors, he would want to draw closer to Jesus, not further away. This man will also need the Lord's help to heal the underlying emotional wounds that would be allowing demonic spirits to access his life.

If the words of the Saint Louis de Montfort consecration vow helped the man to acknowledge his sinfulness and directed him to the Blessed Trinity for healing, then this vow would be a great benefit. Instead of directing a person to the Blessed Trinity, the words of this vow state, *"There is nothing in me which does not merit Thine anger and Thy repulse, I dare no more come by myself before Thy Most Holy and August Majesty. It is on this account that I have recourse to the intercession of Thy most holy Mother, whom Thou hast given me for a mediatrix with Thee. It is by her means that I hope to obtain of Thee contrition, and the pardon of my sins."*[8]

If the man with the pornography addiction said to God, "I dare no more come before Thy Most Holy and August Majesty," then demonic spirits would have the right to hinder that man's relationship with God. Whenever this man felt like turning to God in prayer, the demonic spirits would remind him about his own words that he made in this vow. They would say to him, "You cannot turn to God for help! There's nothing in you that does not merit God's anger and repulse!"

Another part of this vow that demonic spirits could use to hinder a person's salvation comes from the statement that says, "It is by her means that I hope to obtain of Thee contrition, and the pardon of my sins." Although the Blessed Mother may be one of the Church's greatest saints, she does not have the ability to forgive sins. It is not possible for Mary to grant salvation or to pardon a person's sins.

In the event that the man with the pornography addiction tried turning to Mary for the forgiveness of his sin, he would be choosing a false form of salvation. According to John 14:6, Jesus says, *"I am the way, and the truth, and the life. No one comes to the Father except through me."* According to Mary's own words in the Magnificat, she said, *"My spirit rejoices in God my Savior, for he has looked with favor on the lowliness of his servant."*[9]

The only way for the man with the pornography addiction to enter heaven is to turn to Jesus for the forgiveness of his sins. When a man turns to Jesus with a true act of contrition and sincerity of heart, the Lord will help that man break free from the bondage of evil, so that he can start working in partnership with the Holy Spirit to accomplish God's will in his life. Because demonic spirits want to keep this man away from an authentic relationship with God, they can use the words of this vow against him for his eternal destruction.

Another disturbing part of this consecration vow is that it gives an unknown spiritual entity the right to dispose of a person's soul any way it wants, without exception. The words of the vow read as follows: *"In the presence of all the heavenly court I choose thee this day for my Mother and Mistress. I deliver and consecrate to thee, as thy slave, my body and soul, my goods, both interior and exterior, and even the value of all my good actions, past, present and future; leaving to you the entire and full right of disposing of me, and all that belongs to me, without exception."*[10]

If the man with the pornography addiction entered into this spiritually binding agreement, he would be giving his *Mother and Mistress* all these rights. If the man were to give all these rights to the Blessed Mother, then this vow would be in direct conflict with the teachings of the Catholic Church. According to the Catechism in section 450, *From the beginning of Christian history, the assertion of Christ's lordship over the world and over history has implicitly recognized that man should not submit his personal freedom in an absolute manner to any earthly power, but only to God the Father and the Lord Jesus Christ.*

Because the words of this vow don't specifically identify the type of spiritual entity that has been chosen as a person's *Mother and Mistress,* it's possible for the same demonic entities that were operating under the name *Queen of Heaven* in Jeremiah 44, to assume that role. This vow has the potential to be dangerous because whatever type of spiritual entity that wants to operate under the name *Mother and Mistress* holds the right to dispose of a person's soul, along with all their good deeds, both interior and exterior, without exception.

A good example of the way demonic entities can operate under any religious-sounding name they want comes from the Jewish exiles who were living in the land of Egypt. When God sent the prophet Jeremiah to them he said, *"Thus says the Lord of hosts, the God of Israel: You yourselves have seen all the disaster that I have brought on Jerusalem and on all the towns of Judah. Look at them; today they are a desolation, without an inhabitant in them, because of the wickedness that they committed, provoking me to anger, in that they went to make offerings and serve other gods that they had not known, neither they, nor you, nor your ancestors. Yet I persistently sent to you all my servants the prophets, saying, 'I beg you not to do this abominable thing that I hate!'"[11]*

Then all the men who were aware that their wives had been making offerings to other gods, and all the women who stood by, a great assembly, all the people who lived in Pathros in the land of Egypt, answered Jeremiah: "As for the word that you have spoken to us in the name of the Lord, we are not going to listen to you. Instead, we will do everything that we have vowed, make offerings to the queen of heaven and pour out libations to her."[12]

Because the demons that had been operating under the name *Queen of Heaven* had been giving these people special powers, they could not break free. In response to Jeremiah's warning they said, *"We used to have plenty of food, and prospered, and saw no misfortune. But from the time we stopped making offerings to the queen of heaven and pouring out libations to her, we have lacked everything and have perished by the sword and by famine."*

And the women said, "Indeed we will go on making offerings to the queen of heaven and pouring out libations to her; do you think that we made cakes for her, marked with her image, and poured out libations to her without our husbands' being involved?"[13]

Because these people refused to stop worshiping the demonic spirits that were operating under the name *Queen of Heaven,* the Lord declared to them, *"I am going to watch over them for harm and not for good; all the people of Judah who are in the land of Egypt shall perish by the sword and by famine, until not one is left."[14]* After all these people had been destroyed, the demonic spirits didn't die with them, they simply changed their names and began making more sinful agreements with other people in different geographical locations.

The same demonic entities that were operating under the name *Queen of Heaven* in Egypt also had the ability to operate under different religious-sounding names in other parts of the world. In the Babylonian and Assyrian culture they were using the name of Ishtar. In the Greek culture they were operating under the name of Aphrodite. In the Egyptian culture they were known as Isis. Worship of the female goddess was first introduced by King Manasseh in 2 Kings 21:1–7 after he set up an Asherah pole in the house of the Lord, and continued under the name of Artemis for the Ephesians.

In today's culture, the same demonic entities continue their assault against humanity. In the New Age movement these demonic entities operate under the names of Isis, Ascended Master Mary, the Great Enchantress, Goddess of Magic, Queen of the Gods, Star of the Sea, Goddess of Love and Our Lady of Light. Because demonic entities can operate under any religious-sounding name they want, it becomes very dangerous to sell your soul along with the value of all your good deeds to any spiritual entity other than the Blessed Trinity.

In the event that you have entered into a consecration vow, or made any other type of spiritually binding agreement, you may want to take some time right now to ask the Holy Spirit to shine the light of truth deep into your heart to discern the reasons why. Were you frightened of Jesus and felt that there was nothing in your life that didn't merit the Lord's *anger and repulse?* Or were you hoping that your *Mother and Mistress* could forgive your sins and obtain favor for you with the Blessed Trinity?

Did you enter into a thirty-three-day consecration in an attempt to take a spiritual shortcut to God instead of spending time developing an authentic relationship with Jesus? Another point you may want to consider is if you already had an authentic relationship with Jesus, why would you want to choose an alternative form of salvation?

If you discover an unhealthy motive after making any kind of spiritually binding agreement, you may want to take a moment to denounce those vows in the name, power and authority of Jesus.

If you were trying to make a deal with God in an attempt to get something that you wanted, you may want to pray, Dear Heavenly Father, please forgive me for offering my _____ in exchange for _____. I break those agreements right now in the name, power and authority of Jesus. I command any evil spirits that have attached themselves to me, or have oppressed me in any way, to depart now, and go straight to Jesus Christ for him to deal with as he wills.

Dear Lord Jesus, Please forgive me for making vows and agreements with unknown spiritual entities. I realize now that you want my full devotion, and I hereby surrender my life into your service. Please purify and cleanse my life, and remove anything evil or demonic from me, so that I may serve you both now and forevermore.

In the event that you have made a consecration vow with impure motives, you may want to pray, Dear Heavenly Father, please forgive me for choosing an alternative form of salvation, and for selling my soul along with the value of my good deeds to unknown spiritual entities. I break those vows and agreements right now in the name, power and authority of Jesus.

I command and bid all the powers who molest me—by the power of the Lord God Almighty, in the name of Jesus Christ my Savior—to leave me forever, and to be consigned into the everlasting lake of fire, that they may never again touch me or any other creature in the entire world.

Dear Lord Jesus, please send forth the power of your Holy Spirit to purify my mind, heart, soul and emotions.

May your precious blood cleanse every area of my life that has been vacated by the presence of darkness. Please destroy any evil spirits that have attached themselves to me or my family members because of these vows, and cleanse us with the fire of your all-consuming love. I invite you into my heart, Lord Jesus, and enthrone you as my Lord and Savior for all eternity. Amen.

THE SIN OF IDOLATRY OCCURS IN THE HEART

When most people think of the sin of idolatry, they may picture a primitive statue of a pagan god surrounded by worshipers who want something from the spiritual realm. If the statue represented a carved image of a healing god, the worshipers may want healing. If the statue resembled the grim reaper wearing a long robe and holding a sickle in his hand, the worshipers may be criminals who want Santa Muerte's protection from the police.

Although the worship of carved wooden, plastic or ceramic statues may be a good example of idol worship, the sin of idolatry has a much broader definition. According to the Catechism in section 2113, *Idolatry not only refers to false pagan worship. It remains a constant temptation to faith. Idolatry consists in divinizing what is not God. Man commits idolatry whenever he honors and reveres a creature in place of God.*

A good example of how the sin of idolatry works comes from the life of a wealthy man named Anthony. Although Anthony grew up in a good Catholic home and attended daily Mass, he had a desire to grow rich. Every day Anthony would attend daily Mass and pray for God to make his business endeavors prosper. In his prayer time Anthony would say, "Oh God, please help me close this deal. Oh God, please help me find a buyer for that property. Oh God, I need to borrow more money with a lower interest rate."

When God created Anthony's soul, he placed at the center of his heart an altar for worship. The altar that resides deep within Anthony's heart only has room for one God. It's not possible to worship the Lord and at the same time worship the false god of money. Jesus makes this point clear in Matthew 6:24, by saying, *"No one can serve two masters; for a slave will either hate the one and love the other, or be devoted to the one and despise the other. You cannot serve God and wealth."*

Although Anthony was aware of this Scripture passage, he never thought the pursuit of money could be a false god in his life or a form of idol worship. Anthony considered himself to be a hard-working Catholic businessman who loved the Lord. If you waved a hundred dollar bill before Anthony's eyes and asked him to bow down and worship, he would refuse. Yet deep inside his heart, there was room for only one God. On the altar of Anthony's heart, there could either be a golden dollar sign or the Lord, Jesus Christ.

The determining factor would be how Anthony lived his life. Did Anthony spend his time serving the Lord in the mission field, or did Anthony spend his time conducting business deals for the purpose of making more money? Because the altar of Anthony's heart remained hidden from other people to see, it was very easy for Anthony to maintain a perception of holiness, while at the same time, serving the false god of money.

Anthony began to realize the meaning of the Lord's teaching about serving two masters after he experienced a major stock market loss. Within the first few hours, Anthony's brokerage account was down eight thousand dollars. Instead of selling his positions and taking the loss, Anthony wanted to wait for a turnaround, but every day the market continued moving lower. When it was all over, Anthony had lost hundreds of thousands of dollars. He was devastated. All the proceeds from his high-pressure business deals where he had fought with buyers and bankers to make the maximum amount of profit buying and selling real estate had vanished before his eyes.

After losing many years of his life that had been spent acquiring the money, Anthony found himself in a deep state of depression. The golden dollar sign that he placed upon the altar of his heart had been shattered into a thousand pieces. With nowhere else to turn, Anthony fell to his knees and sought the Lord with all his heart. As he cried out to the Lord, he said from the depths of his soul, "I will do whatever you want from here on out."

As soon as Anthony made a complete surrender to the Lord, he was flooded with the peaceful presence of the Holy Spirit and received his first missionary assignment. As soon as Anthony began serving the Lord, he realized how he had been serving the false god of money for most of his life. The most profound realization occurred in Anthony's prayer life. Instead of praying, "Oh God, please do this because I want more money," Anthony began praying, "Oh God, what do you want me to do today?"

Instead of having the golden dollar sign on the altar of his heart with God somewhere in the background, God was now ruling and reigning in Anthony's heart, and money was somewhere in the background. In a way, Anthony went from being self-employed to being God-employed. After removing the false god of money from his life, Anthony began to realize why it's impossible for a man to serve two masters.

According to Sacred Scripture, the sin of greed has been described as a form of idolatry. For example, in Colossians 3:5–6, Saint Paul says, *"Put to death, therefore, whatever in you is earthly: fornication, impurity, passion, evil desire, and greed (which is idolatry). On account of these the wrath of God is coming on those who are disobedient."* Saint Paul makes the same point in Ephesians 5:5, by saying, *"Be sure of this, that no fornicator or impure person, or one who is greedy (that is, an idolater), has any inheritance in the kingdom of Christ and of God."*

Not only is greed considered a form of idolatry, but there are many other false gods mentioned in the Bible that can also be a form of idol worship within a person's heart. Basically anything a person places on the altar of his or her heart, other than the Blessed Trinity, can become a false god and a form of idol worship.

Another example of idolatry comes from a woman named Lisa who placed her husband and children upon the altar of her heart. Because Lisa's family was the primary focus of her life, the Lord was forced to take a second place position. Even though Lisa prayed and attended church on Sunday, her entire life revolved around making her husband happy. Because Lisa would do anything for her family, her husband began to take advantage of his wife's love and devotion. Lisa eventually found herself making all the compromises in an attempt to give her husband everything he wanted.

Because Lisa's husband didn't need to accomplish any kind of emotional healing work or personal growth to keep his marriage healthy, he eventually grew more distant from Lisa's love. The more Lisa tried to love and serve her husband, the more it pushed him away. Eventually Lisa's husband had an affair with a younger woman from his office, and her marriage ended in divorce.

During this time Lisa was overwhelmed with grief. She spent the next several months locked inside her home, refusing to eat as she grieved her losses. With nowhere else to turn, Lisa offered God the rightful place within her heart. After making Jesus the Lord of her life, she realized her mistake—instead of allowing God to rule upon the altar of her heart, she had given that sacred place of worship to a sinful man who was constantly letting her down.

After Lisa realized the difference between placing God at the center of her heart, with her family kneeling around the altar, and placing her family upon the altar, with God in the background, she finally realized the importance of the Lord's teaching in Matthew 10:37–38, when Jesus said, *"Whoever loves father or mother more than me is not worthy of me; and whoever loves son or daughter more than me is not worthy of me; and whoever does not take up the cross and follow me is not worthy of me."*

Another example of idolatry has been described in 1 Corinthians 10:14, when Saint Paul said, *"Therefore, my dear friends, flee from the worship of idols."* After explaining the danger of eating food that had been sacrificed to idols, Saint Paul said, *"What do I imply then? That food sacrificed to idols is anything, or that an idol is anything? No, I imply that what pagans sacrifice, they sacrifice to demons and not to God. I do not want you to be partners with demons."[1]*

Although all sin is an open door for demonic oppression, the sin of idolatry is far more serious because it gives demons direct access to the sacred place of worship within a person's heart. For example, when a man places a statue of Santa Muerte on the altar of his heart and commits the sin of idolatry, the demons will have direct access to that man's spiritual life. Once demons are allowed to interact with a man through his sacred place of worship, they will hinder his ability to maintain an authentic relationship with the Blessed Trinity.

Although it may be easy to see the dangers in praying to false pagan objects such as Santa Muerte, what some people fail to understand is that the sin of idolatry occurs within a person's heart, and it has nothing to do with the shape, size or color of the statue. For example, in the same way that it would be possible to commit the sin of idolatry with a statue of Santa Muerte, it would also be possible to commit the sin of idolatry with a statue of the Blessed Mother.

Because idol worship is not limited to the shape, size or color of the statue, the only way a man or woman would know if he or she has committed the sin of idolatry would be to ask the Holy Spirit to shine the light of truth deep into his or her heart. For example, one woman may have the Lord Jesus at the center of her heart, with Mary at her side praying before the altar as an intercessor; while another woman may have the Blessed Mother on center stage, hoping that Mary will grant her salvation because of her daily devotions to the Rosary.

Another way to determine if you have been committing the sin of idolatry is to look at anything in your life that you have been turning to for blessings, protection or salvation, other than the Blessed Trinity. For example, if a woman has a strong devotion to Padre Pio and wears Padre Pio charm bracelets and has many Padre Pio crosses and medallions that she uses for protection (similar to using a talisman or amulet for protection), but is constantly complaining about being attacked by the devil, it may be a good indicator that she has been turning to Padre Pio for protection, instead of trusting in the Lord, Jesus Christ.

If that were the case, her so-called Padre Pio devotions may be considered a form of idol worship, and as a false form of protection, those devotions would be the source the demons were using to access her life. In order to break free, the woman would need to remove the chains from around her neck, remove Padre Pio from the altar of her heart, and repent of the sin of idolatry. After repenting of the sin of idolatry, she would need to spend time developing an authentic relationship with the Blessed Trinity.

In the event that you have been experiencing demonic oppression, you may want to spend some time in prayer right now asking the Holy Spirit to shine the light of truth deep inside your heart to show you the source of the problem. A good prayer to begin this process would be, Dear Heavenly Father, please send forth the power of your Holy Spirit to illuminate every area of my life and heart where I have chosen to serve false gods, instead of serving you.

Please forgive me for offering the sacred place of worship within my heart to anything other than you, the one true God. Please convict me of all my sins, especially the sin of idolatry, and give me the grace to see my sins the same way that you see them.

Please help me to identify any false gods in my life that I have placed upon the altar of my heart, so that with your grace, I may remove them. I give you permission to remove any false gods from my life, so that you can take your rightful place of worship at the center of my heart. Amen.

BEWARE OF DEMONIC RELIGIOUS SPIRITS

When most people think of demonic spirits, they envision a sinister presence of darkness that drives a person into total depravity, or an ugly looking monster that incites people to commit violent crimes. Although these definitions are certainly true, the devil also has the ability to disguise his true identity and appear as a beautiful angel of light.

When Saint Paul was describing a group of religious leaders who appeared good and holy on the outside, but inwardly were ravenous wolves, he said, *"For such boasters are false apostles, deceitful workers, disguising themselves as apostles of Christ. And no wonder! Even Satan disguises himself as an angel of light. So it is not strange if his ministers also disguise themselves as ministers of righteousness."*[1]

If the devil cannot ensnare a person's soul with sexual perversion, violent crimes and total depravity, then his alternative method of attack would be to appear as an angel of light to help people practice religion. Because Satan and his vast army of fallen angels had spent thousands of years in heaven worshiping God, they are very familiar with authentic forms of worship. They know exactly what is pleasing to God and what is an unacceptable form of worship.

If the devil can trick a person into participating in an unacceptable form of worship, then he can hinder that person's relationship with God. A good example of how the devil can influence religious worship comes from the lives of the Pharisees. Although the Pharisees were highly respected religious leaders, the devil had the ability to keep them so focused on the external practice of religion that they failed to recognize the divinity of Christ in their very presence.

One way the devil was able to attack the Pharisees was to fill their hearts with spiritual pride. Instead of trying to hinder the religious leader's daily devotions, demonic spirits wanted to inspire these men to lift up lofty prayers, so that other people would notice them and honor them with terms of respect. That way, the Pharisees would want *to have the place of honor at banquets and the best seats in the synagogues, and to be greeted with respect in the marketplaces.*[2]

Demonic spirits of religion also wanted to help the Pharisees engage in contentious theological arguments. Demonic spirits wanted to make these men feel intellectually superior to everybody else, as if their knowledge about God was more important than an obedient relationship with God. Instead of allowing the scribes and Pharisees to enter into a loving relationship with Jesus, demonic spirits kept these men so busy and blinded with the practice of religion that they started telling lies about Jesus so that they could have him arrested.

Even though Jesus performed many miracles to establish his identity as the Messiah, the minds and hearts of these religious leaders had become so darkened that they started looking for an opportunity to kill Jesus. After making many attempts to reach out to the scribes and Pharisees, Jesus eventually condemned their actions by saying, *"Woe to you, scribes and Pharisees, hypocrites! For you lock people out of the kingdom of heaven. For you do not go in yourselves, and when others are going in, you stop them. Woe to you, scribes and Pharisees, hypocrites! For you cross sea and land to make a single convert, and you make the new convert twice as much a child of hell as yourselves. You snakes, you brood of vipers! How can you escape being sentenced to hell?"³*

After an entire generation of religious leaders who had Jesus crucified on the cross of Calvary had passed away, the demonic religious spirits that had been driving their behaviors didn't die with them; they simply changed their names and began helping other people practice religion. Satan has an entire division of fallen angels in his vast army that specializes in helping people practice religion. Once these deceptive religious spirits enter a person's life, they will focus that person's attention on the external practice of religion, making it more important than entering into an authentic relationship with the Blessed Trinity.

Satan uses this strategy because he knows that if he can prevent a person from establishing an authentic relationship with Jesus, that person may never accomplish the Lord's will in his or her life. In the event that a person never accomplishes the Lord's will in his or her life, that person may hear the Lord say on the last day, *"I never knew you; go away from me, you evildoers."⁴* In the event a person hears the Lord making this statement, that man or woman runs the risk of being eternally separated from God for all eternity.

Because this is one of the devil's preferred methods of ensnaring religious souls, it may be helpful to study the Lord's teaching in further detail. According to Matthew 7:21–23, Jesus said, *"Not everyone who says to me, 'Lord, Lord,' will enter the kingdom of heaven, but only the one who does the will of my Father in heaven. On that day many will say to me, 'Lord, Lord, did we not prophesy in your name, and cast out demons in your name, and do many deeds of power in your name?' Then I will declare to them, 'I never knew you; go away from me, you evildoers.'"*

In this Scripture passage, Jesus is describing the Day of Judgment. He is addressing a group of believers who appear to be Christians. These people consider Jesus to be their Lord, and they even call him, "Lord, Lord." We also see that these people spoke prophesies in the Lord's name, cast out demons in the Lord's name and even worked many deeds of power in the Lord's name, yet Jesus declares to them, *"I never knew you."*[5]

The type of *knowing* that Jesus is describing is an intimate knowing between two lovers, the obedient knowing between a servant and his Master, and the authentic knowing that only comes from a lifelong relationship. Although these people knew who Jesus was, and although they spent a lifetime performing deeds of power in his name, they never really entered into an authentic relationship with Jesus.

Another reason why these people were *not* allowed to enter heaven was that they never accomplished the Father's will in their lives. God has a specific purpose and plan for everybody's life. The only way to know God's specific purpose and plan for your life is to maintain an authentic relationship with Jesus. It is through an authentic relationship with Jesus that we can work in partnership with the Holy Spirit to accomplish the Father's will for our lives.

Because the devil knows how important it is for people to work in partnership with the Holy Spirit to accomplish the Father's will in their lives, he will do everything in his power to distract people with the external practice of religion, so that they never enter into an authentic relationship with Jesus.

If the devil can get a man to spend his entire lifetime practicing religion, there's a good chance he will never enter into an authentic relationship with Jesus. When a man fails to enter into an authentic relationship with Jesus, he may never accomplish God's specific purpose and plan for his life. In the event that a man never accomplishes God's specific purpose and plan for his life, he may hear the Lord say on the last day, *"I never knew you; go away from me, you evildoers."*[6]

Because demonic religious spirits have a long history of helping people practice religion, and are very good at disguising themselves as angels of light, you may want to spend some time in prayer asking the Lord to shine the light of truth deep within your heart to see if you have ever made agreements with demonic religious spirits that may be preventing you from developing an authentic relationship with Jesus.

One way to know if you have made agreements with demonic religious spirits that could be hindering your relationship with Jesus is to ask yourself a few simple questions. For example, have you completely surrendered your life into the Lord's service?

According to 1 John 2:5–6, *By this we may be sure that we are in him: whoever says, "I abide in him," ought to walk just as he walked.* Are you walking hand-in-hand with Jesus, the Lover of your soul?

According to John 14:23, Jesus says, *"Those who love me will keep my word, and my Father will love them, and we will come to them and make our home with them."* Have you filled your spiritual house with the all-consuming love of the Blessed Trinity?

In John 10:27, Jesus says, *"My sheep hear my voice. I know them, and they follow me."* Are you able to listen to and discern the Good Shepherd's softly spoken voice in your prayer time, and do you follow him in complete obedience?

According to 1 John 2:4–5, *Whoever says, "I have come to know him," but does not obey his commandments, is a liar, and in such a person the truth does not exist; but whoever obeys his word, truly in this person the love of God has reached perfection.* Do you read Sacred Scripture on a regular basis for the purpose of incorporating God's commandments, teachings and truth into your life?

According to 1 John 4:13, *By this we know that we abide in him and he in us, because he has given us of his Spirit.* Have you been working in partnership with the Holy Spirit to accomplish the Lord's will in your life?

According to John 15:1–2, Jesus says, *"I am the true vine, and my Father is the vinegrower. He removes every branch in me that bears no fruit. Every branch that bears fruit he prunes to make it bear more fruit."* How has God been purifying your life so that you can produce more fruit for the kingdom of heaven?

According to John 15:4–5, Jesus says, *"Abide in me as I abide in you. Just as the branch cannot bear fruit by itself unless it abides in the vine, neither can you unless you abide in me. I am the vine, you are the branches. Those who abide in me and I in them bear much fruit, because apart from me you can do nothing."* Have you been working in partnership with the Blessed Trinity to advance God's kingdom and to fulfill the Great Commission?

According to 1 John 5:10–12, *Those who believe in the Son of God have the testimony in their hearts. Those who do not believe in God have made him a liar by not believing in the testimony that God has given concerning his Son. And this is the testimony: God gave us eternal life, and this life is in his Son. Whoever has the Son has life; whoever does not have the Son of God does not have life.* Does the life-giving presence of Jesus dwell in your heart?

INTERACTION WITH FALLEN ANGELS OF LIGHT

One day the Lord sent Archangel Gabriel to deliver an important message to the prophet Daniel. Because Satan didn't want Daniel to receive the message, he issued a command for the demonic principality that ruled over the region of Persia to fight against him. Once the demonic principality received Satan's orders, thousands of fallen angels surrounded Gabriel and fought against him for three weeks.

The battle probably looked similar to a scene from the movie *The Matrix Reloaded* where Neo found himself fighting an agent that had the ability to reproduce more copies of himself. At first Neo started out fighting ten agents, but because the main antagonist kept reproducing more copies of himself, Neo found himself fighting thirty agents at the same time. When Neo overpowered one opponent, another one would take his place.

In the same way, the battle between Archangel Gabriel and the demonic principality of Persia looked very similar. Gabriel was probably covered with fallen angels. As soon as Gabriel overpowered one demon and cast him aside, another demonic entity would take his place. Because Gabriel was under heavy attack for three weeks, the Lord sent Michael the Archangel to offer some assistance.

As soon as Michael arrived, he engaged the battle and fought against the prince of Persia, so that Gabriel could escape and deliver the message to Daniel. All during this time, Daniel had been praying and fasting. According to Daniel 10:2–3, *At that time I, Daniel, had been mourning for three weeks. I had eaten no rich food, no meat or wine had entered my mouth, and I had not anointed myself at all, for the full three weeks.*

When Gabriel arrived to deliver the prophetic message, Daniel described the encounter by saying, *"I looked up and saw a man clothed in linen, with a belt of gold from Uphaz around his waist. His body was like beryl, his face like lightning, his eyes like flaming torches, his arms and legs like the gleam of burnished bronze, and the sound of his words like the roar of a multitude.*[1]

"When I heard the sound of his words, I fell into a trance, face to the ground. But then a hand touched me and roused me to my hands and knees. He said to me, 'Daniel, greatly beloved, pay attention to the words that I am going to speak to you. Stand on your feet, for I have now been sent to you.' So while he was speaking this word to me, I stood up trembling.

"He said to me, 'Do not fear, Daniel, for from the first day that you set your mind to gain understanding and to humble yourself before your God, your words have been heard, and I have come because of your words. But the prince of the kingdom of Persia opposed me twenty-one days. So Michael, one of the chief princes, came to help me, and I left him there with the prince of the kingdom of Persia, and have come to help you understand what is to happen to your people at the end of days. For there is a further vision for those days.'"[2]

After Gabriel delivered the prophetic message and helped Daniel understand what was to take place concerning the end of days, he needed to get back and help Michael with the battle. In Daniel 10:20–21, after Gabriel finished delivering the message, he said, *"Now I must return to fight against the prince of Persia, and when I am through with him, the prince of Greece will come. But I am to tell you what is inscribed in the book of truth. There is no one with me who contends against these princes except Michael, your prince."*

By studying Daniel's encounter with the Archangel Gabriel, we are provided a great deal of insight into the spiritual realm. First of all, we get a glimpse into Satan's kingdom to see how he divides his territory into different geographical regions. One of Satan's principalities had been established in Persia and another one was located in Greece. Because the Persian principality had dominion over Babylon (where Daniel was living), the demons in that region would probably use different tactics to ensnare souls than the demons in Greece.

We can also see in this situation that even the highest-ranking archangels are limited in their powers and abilities. For example, angels are not omnipresent. They cannot be in two different places at the same time. When Gabriel was fighting the demonic principality in Persia, he was not able to deliver a prophetic message to Daniel during the same time. We also see that angels are not all-powerful. Even though Gabriel wanted to break free from the battle and deliver the message to Daniel, he was prevented from doing so because he was outnumbered and overpowered.

We can also see from Sacred Scripture that angels are sent by God to accomplish a specific purpose.

Gabriel was sent by God to deliver a message to Daniel, but because his efforts had been hindered for three weeks, God sent Michael to assist in the battle.

Other passages of Scripture that confirm how angels are sent by God to accomplish a specific purpose would include Hebrews 1:14, which says, *Are not all angels spirits in the divine service, sent to serve for the sake of those who are to inherit salvation?*

Because angels are God's servants, sent to accomplish a specific purpose in the lives of those who are to inherit salvation, we are *not* allowed to worship them. A good example of why it would be inappropriate for one of God's servants to offer any kind of worship to another of God's servants comes from the Book of Revelation.

After the Apostle John received the visions contained in the Book of Revelation, it's understandable why he would want to express his appreciation. Instead of offering his praise and worship to God, he made a mistake and tried to offer his appreciation to one of his fellow servants. According to Revelation 22:8–9, *I, John, am the one who heard and saw these things. And when I heard and saw them, I fell down to worship at the feet of the angel who showed them to me; but he said to me, "You must not do that! I am a fellow servant with you and your comrades the prophets, and with those who keep the words of this book. Worship God!"*

Because we are only allowed to worship God, it would make sense that all of our prayers should be directed to God. The Catechism makes this point clear in section 2664, by saying, *There is no other way of Christian prayer than Christ. Whether our prayer is communal or personal, vocal or interior, it has access to the Father only if we pray in the name of Jesus.*

When a person tries to offer prayers to Saint Michael the Archangel, it becomes a problem for several reasons. First of all there is only one archangel named Michael. He is not omnipresent and he cannot be in two different places at the same time. If God issued an order for Michael to fight against the demonic principality of Persia so that Gabriel could break free, he might be there for three weeks. During this time, he would not be available to answer millions of other prayer requests.

In a more modern-day example, let's say that God gave Saint Michael the Archangel an assignment to prevent a nuclear war from occurring between North Korea and the United States. Because there is only one Saint Michael the Archangel, he cannot be in two different places at the same time. Because Saint Michael is not omnipresent, it would not be possible for him to answer all the prayer requests from the people living in Venezuela, while answering prayer requests from people living in Mexico, while at the same time, accomplishing God's assignment in North Korea.

Because Saint Michael the Archangel is limited in his ability to answer and fulfill prayer requests, it would make more sense to pray directly to Jesus, the Commander of the angelic army. That way, the Commander could issue an order to one of his available servants. If the Commander wanted Saint Michael to minister to an elderly lady from New York because her cat was stuck in a tree, he could issue a command, and because Saint Michael is an obedient servant of God, he would obey the command and help rescue the elderly lady's cat. If Saint Michael was busy on assignment in North Korea, the Commander might want to send a different angel to help rescue the elderly lady's cat.

Another reason why it's dangerous to pray directly to angelic beings is that Satan can assign religious-sounding names to his vast army of fallen angels. For example, let's say a man from Afghanistan started praying to his guardian angel for assistance. If that man was not praying to God in Jesus' name, then according to the Catechism in section 2664, his prayer would not have any access to God. If the man from Afghanistan wasn't praying to God, then the devil would have the right to assign religious-sounding names to his vast army of fallen angels so that they could answer the man's prayer request.

Another reason why it's dangerous to pray directly to angelic beings comes from a woman named Sandy who paid fifty dollars to attend a New Age seminar entitled, "Meet your Angels." During this class, a psychic introduced Sandy to a demonic spirit named Archangel Uriel. The psychic convinced Sandy that Archangel Uriel was her best friend, and that Uriel wanted to watch over her and provide her with an abundance of blessings.

As soon as Sandy started praying to her so-called guardian angel, all kinds of demonic attacks began occurring in her life. Although Sandy complained about experiencing energy that burned like fire that had manifested in her body so badly that she could hardly walk, she remained convinced that Archangel Uriel was still her best friend and that he was trying to help her break free from whatever it was that was attacking her.

In the event that you have been praying to unknown spiritual entities or fallen angelic beings of light, you may want to denounce those practices in the name, power and authority of Jesus. A good prayer to begin this process would be, Dear Heavenly Father, please forgive me for all the times I have prayed to demonic spirits instead of praying directly to you. I denounce all forms of communication with demonic spirits in the name, power and authority of Jesus.

If any demonic spirits have attached themselves to me or oppressed me in any way, I bind you evil spirits, demonic forces, satanic powers, principalities and satanic thrones; I bind all kings and princes of terrors, I bind all demonic assignments and functions of destruction, from the air, water, fire, the ground, the netherworld and the evil forces of nature. I bind all enemies of Christ present together, and I command that you leave my life now and go straight to the feet of Jesus Christ. Your assignments and influences are over.

I call forth the Holy Spirit, the heavenly host, the holy angels of God, to surround and protect, and cleanse with God's holy light, all areas vacated by the forces of evil. I ask the Holy Spirit to permeate my mind, heart, body, spirit and soul, creating a hunger and thirst for God's holy Word, and to fill me to overflowing with the life and love of my Lord, Jesus Christ. Amen.

PRAYING TO UNKNOWN SPIRITUAL ENTITIES

One day when Jesus was ministering near the Mediterranean Sea, a Canaanite woman began shouting after him saying, *"Have mercy on me, Lord, Son of David; my daughter is tormented by a demon." But he did not answer her at all. And his disciples came and urged him, saying, "Send her away, for she keeps shouting after us."[1]*

Because the Canaanite woman was persistent in her request, Jesus stopped to engage her in a meaningful conversation. He answered her by saying, *"I was sent only to the lost sheep of the house of Israel."*

But she came and knelt before him, saying, "Lord, help me."

He answered, "It is not fair to take the children's food and throw it to the dogs."

She said, "Yes, Lord, yet even the dogs eat the crumbs that fall from their masters' table."[2]

Because the Canaanite woman was persistent in her request, Jesus answered her by saying, *"Woman, great is your faith! Let it be done for you as you wish." And her daughter was healed instantly.[3]*

In this situation, Jesus didn't want to heal the Canaanite woman's daughter, because the Canaanites worshiped many false gods. When the Canaanite woman went to a pagan temple and prayed to a variety of spiritual entities, she would be making agreements with demonic spirits, and after committing the sin of idolatry, those demonic spirits would have the right to enter her life and attack her children.

Another reason why Jesus didn't want to cast a demonic spirit out of her daughter's life was that the mother would probably return to the same pagan temple and acquire even more demons. In order to address this issue, Jesus needed to define the difference between the lost sheep of the house of Israel and the dogs that take away their food. In order for the Canaanite woman's daughter to receive the healing that she desired, it would be necessary for her to transition out of the kingdom of darkness and into the marvelous light.

In a similar situation, when the daughter of a woman named Jennifer became ill with a mysterious form of illness, she began praying for healing. When her prayers went unanswered, it seemed as if God were distant, too busy, or even worse, that he didn't really care about Jennifer's precious little girl. In an attempt to get God's attention, Jennifer increased her prayer efforts and began asking other people to repeat the same petition, thinking that if twenty people prayed the same prayer, God would grant her request.

When that didn't work, Jennifer began looking for more powerful intercessors. Because Jennifer had a deep devotion to the Blessed Mother, she began praying to the Black Madonna. When that didn't work, she began praying to Our Lady of Lourdes, Our Lady of Fátima and Our Lady of Emmitsburg, all at the same time.

When that didn't bring the desired results, she began praying to Saint Jude, the patron of desperate causes, and Saint Peregrine, the miraculous healer of cancer.

Because the little girl's condition continued to grow worse, Jennifer became very desperate and took her daughter to see a psychic healer. During the session, the psychic healer called upon the Ascended Master Mother Mary, imparted spiritual healing energy and anointed her daughter with a rose-scented oil. Because Jennifer noticed a slight improvement in her daughter's condition, she visited several other psychic healers, and even took her daughter to see a Reiki practitioner.

Eventually Jennifer found herself swept away by the New Age movement. Although her daughter's condition showed a few signs of improvement, similar to the way a rubber ball would make new highs while bouncing down a set of stairs, none of the New Age techniques could provide any lasting results, and her daughter's condition eventually spiraled downward. Because Jennifer had spent thousands of dollars, and many years of her life crying out to God for help without seeing any results, she found herself angry, bitter and very disappointed with God.

One reason why Jennifer didn't receive the instant healing that she desired comes from the Ten Commandments. According to Exodus 20:4–6, God said, *"You shall not make for yourself an idol, whether in the form of anything that is in heaven above, or that is on the earth beneath, or that is in the water under the earth. You shall not bow down to them or worship them; for I the Lord your God am a jealous God, punishing children for the iniquity of parents, to the third and the fourth generation of those who reject me, but showing steadfast love to the thousandth generation of those who love me and keep my commandments."*

In the event that Jennifer committed the sin of idolatry by praying to unknown spiritual entities that would give her anything she wanted, demonic spirits would have the right to answer her prayer request. Once Jennifer committed the sin of idolatry, demonic spirits would have the right to attack her children. The reason God would allow demons to attack a person's child is because parents hold a form of spiritual authority over their children. For example, if God allowed a mother's holiness to cover her children with a blessing of protection, then in the same way, a mother's agreements with demonic spirits would also have a negative impact on her children.

The same spiritual concept also applies to infant Baptism. If a mother can take her child to a Catholic Church and have her infant baptized, and if during the Baptism the child receives *an indelible spiritual sign, the character, which consecrates the baptized person for Christian worship,*[4] then in the same way, an occult member could consecrate her child to the devil, and by doing so, the child would receive a demonic impartation. If God allows an infant to receive the Holy Spirit during Baptism, he will also allow a child to receive a demonic impartation during a satanic ritual.

Because parents hold a form of spiritual authority over their children, God would allow the parent's spiritual blessings or curses to affect their children. It is for this reason that God describes himself by saying, *"I the Lord your God am a jealous God, punishing children for the iniquity of parents, to the third and the fourth generation of those who reject me, but showing steadfast love to the thousandth generation of those who love me and keep my commandments."[5]*

Even though this Scripture passage includes a very serious warning by saying, *punishing children for the iniquity of parents,[6]* it's important to understand that God does not punish little children—we punish ourselves by praying to false gods and allowing demonic spirits to enter our lives. Once demonic spirits are allowed to operate in a person's life through the sin of idolatry, those demons would have the right to attack a person's children and cause mysterious forms of illness that no doctor could properly diagnose.

In order for Jennifer to break free from the demonic oppression that was attacking her daughter, she first needed to understand how the sin of idolatry works and why the sin of idolatry is wrong. After Jennifer spent a lot of time denouncing all the sinful agreements that she made visiting psychic healers, she also needed to learn the correct way to pray in communion with the saints to God. Contrary to everything that Jennifer had been taught, Catholics do *not* have the right to pray to anything they want in an attempt to get whatever they want.

The correct way to pray in communion with the saints has been described in the Catechism under a section entitled, "The Way of Prayer."[7] Because all of our prayers need to be focused on God, the Catechism defines the *Blessed Trinity* as God the Father, the Lord Jesus Christ and the Holy Spirit. Now that we have defined the Blessed Trinity, it's important to understand the correct meaning for the word *saint*. The word *saint* means a person who is holy, sanctified and set apart for God. The Catechism defines the word *saint* by saying, *The Church, then, is the holy People of God, and her members are called saints.*[8]

Because the word *saint* means a person who is holy, sanctified and set apart for God, there are three groups of saints. There's a group of saints in heaven who can intercede for us, there's a group of saints in purgatory who are being purified, and there's a group of saints here on earth who are still working out their salvation. For example, when Saint Paul wrote his letter to the Ephesians, he addressed it to them by saying, *to the saints who are in Ephesus and are faithful in Christ Jesus.*[9]

When Saint Paul wrote this letter to the saints in Ephesus, he addressed it to the holy men and women who were living in Ephesus. These were ordinary men and women who made a commitment to follow Jesus. Because Jesus calls all of his disciples to holiness, we are all required to put aside our worldly and fleshly ways so that we can be sanctified and set apart for God. Anyone who maintains an authentic relationship with Jesus, and is constantly growing in holiness, is considered by the Catholic Church to be a saint.

Now that we have defined the word *saint,* let's examine the proper way to pray in *communion with the saints to God.* Because a saint is a human being and part of God's creation, it would be inappropriate to pray directly to another human being, whether it was a man, woman or child. The concept of praying in communion with the saints in heaven works the same way as praying in communion with the saints on earth. For example, let's say that during a prayer meeting five men gathered together in a circle and joined hands in one accord as they presented their needs to God.

In this situation, there would be five saints (men who are striving for holiness) who are joined together in unity and presenting their prayer request to God. The same concept would apply to the saints in heaven. The only difference is that the saints in heaven are more purified than the saints on earth. When praying in communion with the saints in heaven, a person's prayer request would still need to be directed to God. For example, instead of five men holding hands in a circle, you may want to envision a man kneeling before God's throne with the Apostles Peter, James, John and Andrew at his side. In this situation, the Apostles (saints in heaven) would be praying together with the man (a saint on earth) and interceding on his behalf.

As you can imagine, a very serious problem would arise in the men's prayer group if one member thought he had the right to start praying to the other members. Just imagine what that would look like, instead of five men praying to God, picture one man dropping to his knees and worshiping the other men in the group, calling out to his fellow humans with a personal prayer request. As you can imagine, the men in the prayer group would *not* accept any kind of worship, nor would they have the ability to grant his prayer request.

In the same way that it would be inappropriate for a human to pray directly to another human, it would also be inappropriate for a human on earth to pray directly to a human in heaven. In the same way that a holy and sanctified human on earth would reject any form of worship, so too would a sanctified human in heaven reject any form of worship. In the same way a human on earth would not have the ability to fulfill a personal prayer request, so too, would a sanctified human in heaven lack the ability to fulfill a prayer request.

Demons on the other hand will jump at the opportunity to fulfill any kind of prayer request, especially when that person doesn't understand the proper way to pray in communion with the saints to God, or when that person isn't even praying to God. When a person isn't praying to God, there's usually some kind of false god set up on the altar of that person's heart, and as soon as that person commits the sin of idolatry by transferring his or her *indestructible notion of God to anything other than God,*[10] then demons would have the right to enter that person's life and cause mysterious forms of illness.

In Jennifer's situation, when she prayed to God, nothing seemed to happen, but when she started praying to unknown spiritual entities that would give her anything she wanted, all kinds of mystical events started occurring. The only problem was that when Jennifer committed the sin of idolatry, demonic spirits had the right to enter her life and attack her daughter's health. The demons didn't want to attack Jennifer directly, because if they did, she might stop praying to them and turn back to the Lord. Instead the demons would rather cause the maximum amount of damage in a person's life, while at the same time remaining hidden.

In the event that you have been praying to unknown spiritual entities in an attempt to get anything you want, it would be helpful to repent of those sins and turn back to the Lord with all your heart. In Jennifer's situation, she had to learn the proper way to pray in communion with the saints to God. She had to denounce all the times that she prayed to unknown spiritual entities in an attempt to get whatever she wanted. Because demonic spirits had found a comfortable home in her daughter's life, they didn't want to leave without a major battle. In order for Jennifer to help her daughter break free, she needed to establish an authentic relationship with Jesus and develop a healthy prayer life.

DEVELOPING A HEALTHY PRAYER LIFE

One of the easiest ways to engage Jesus in a meaningful conversation would be to picture yourself in a boat with Peter, James, John and Andrew. Because all four of these disciples were fishermen, they would have been very comfortable in a boat with Jesus. These men may have gone fishing with Jesus in the early morning hours just to spend time with him on the water while watching the sun rise over the horizon. The Lord's disciples would have been very comfortable talking to Jesus from the depths of their hearts, using everyday language, while asking him important questions about their lives.

Now picture what it would be like if the disciples were in a boat with Jesus enjoying a beautiful sunrise and Jennifer was in the back of the boat chanting rote prayers over and over again. If Jennifer refused to engage the Lord in a meaningful conversation, the disciples may start to wonder why she needed to be with them in the first place. If all Jennifer was doing was disturbing the spiritual atmosphere, the disciples would probably want to treat her the same way they treated the Canaanite woman.

Another lesson that we can learn from the Canaanite woman is that shouting after the Lord's disciples, and repeating the same petition over and over again, may only aggregate the situation. Because an authentic form of prayer with God works like a conversation, where one person talks and the other person listens, it would be more helpful to engage the Lord in a meaningful conversation, instead of chanting the same prayer request over and over again.

Jesus warns us about heaping up empty phrases in Matthew 6:7–8, by saying, *"When you are praying, do not heap up empty phrases as the Gentiles do; for they think that they will be heard because of their many words. Do not be like them, for your Father knows what you need before you ask him."*

The word for repeating vain repetitions in Greek is βατταλογέω, which means to repeat idly or to offer to God meaningless and mechanically repeated phrases. For example, instead of trying to pray a million Rosaries in an attempt to get God to do whatever you want, it would be better to enter into an authentic conversation with the Lord by asking him specific questions about your life and discerning his answers. For example, in Jennifer's situation, she could have asked Jesus to show her the source of her daughter's illness.

Jennifer could have asked the Lord to give her a Bible verse, and after praying, she could have rested in the Sacred Silence and allowed the Holy Spirit to speak to her about her situation. If the Lord gave Jennifer a Scripture passage from 1 Samuel 15:23 that said, *For rebellion is no less a sin than divination, and stubbornness is like iniquity and idolatry,* she could have taken that verse to heart and engaged the Lord in a meaningful conversation. When Jennifer prayed, God would have listened, and if Jennifer took the time to listen and meditate on God's Word, then God could have spoken to her with the words that she needed to hear.

In the event that you have been repeating the same prayer request over and over again, and never receiving an answer from the Lord, you may want to change your prayer life by engaging the Lord in a meaningful conversation. One way to begin this process would be to speak to Jesus directly from your heart. In the same way that Peter, James, John and Andrew spoke to Jesus while inside the boat, you can also picture yourself with them on the Sea of Galilee. Imagine what it would be like to watch the sun rise sitting next to Jesus. Allow yourself to fall into the Lord's loving arms and talk to him about the details of your life.

Another way to enter into a meaningful conversation with the Blessed Trinity would be to pray at a table with four chairs. After taking your place in one of the chairs, picture what it would be like if your Heavenly Father were sitting across from you. In another empty chair, picture Jesus to your right and the Holy Spirit to your left. After you enter into the presence of God, allow yourself to speak to the Blessed Trinity from the depths of a humble and contrite heart.

In an effort to deepen your prayer life, you may want to stop praying to anything other than the Blessed Trinity for the next thirty days. To begin this process, all you need to do is convert all the time you spend praying devotions to the saints into time spent developing a deeper relationship with your Heavenly Father, the Lord Jesus Christ and the Holy Spirit. You may want to make a commitment to spend thirty minutes every evening sitting at a table with four chairs, asking the Blessed Trinity questions about your life, and then spend an additional thirty minutes resting in the Sacred Silence to discern God's answers.

During your prayer time with the Blessed Trinity, it would also be helpful to remember that an authentic form of worship occurs by aligning your will with God's will, not trying to make God give you whatever it is that you want. By developing a deeper relationship with the Blessed Trinity, and aligning your will with God's will, you will be able to receive all the wisdom, knowledge, understanding, direction and insight that you need, along with an abundant outpouring of God's blessings into every area of your life.

THE IMPORTANCE OF EMOTIONAL HEALING

One day when the disciples were sharing a meal together in Capernaum, they began wondering about the people who were conducting business in the shops surrounding the terrace where they were seated. When the disciples noticed a group of Pharisees dressed in brightly colored robes, they asked Jesus, *"Who is the greatest in the kingdom of heaven?"*[1]

Jesus responded by calling a little child over and saying, *"Truly I tell you, unless you change and become like children, you will never enter the kingdom of heaven. Whoever becomes humble like this child is the greatest in the kingdom of heaven."*[2]

As the disciples pondered the meaning of the Lord's answer, they quickly realized all the positive characteristics that are present in little children. The first observation was that little children are completely dependent on their parents, in the same way that we should be dependent on God. Little children are not consumed with worldly ways, but rather they are simple, humble and honest, and it is through these characteristics that a person can enter into an authentic relationship with Jesus.

Little children also operate from their God-given natural programming. They are not born with any natural fears. Newborn babies are not scared of being humiliated in front of other people. Their precious and simple hearts have not been hardened by years of emotional abuse. They are not consumed with a compulsive need to watch sporting events or a desire to take revenge on their enemies. Little children are so pure, simple and loving that they don't need to change to enter the kingdom of heaven; but rather, adults need to change and become more like little children if we want to enter the kingdom of heaven.

Because it's God's desire for everyone to maintain a simplistic purity of heart, it would make sense that the devil would want to attack the purity of our hearts to prevent us from entering the kingdom of heaven. One way the devil is able to attack a person's purity of heart is through the lack of forgiveness. Saint Paul identifies the lack of forgiveness as one of the devil's devices and encourages everyone to forgive, *so that we may not be outwitted by Satan.*[3]

Jesus makes the same point in Matthew 6:14–15, by saying, *"For if you forgive others their trespasses, your heavenly Father will also forgive you; but if you do not forgive others, neither will your Father forgive your trespasses."* Because everybody is required to forgive, it becomes a sin when we refuse to forgive. If the devil can harden our hearts through the lack of forgiveness, causing us to violate one of the Lord's commandments, then he can use that sin against us in an attempt to prevent us from entering the kingdom of heaven.

A good example of how the devil can use the lack of forgiveness to harden our hearts and interfere with our relationship with God comes from an Amish woman named Rachel. When Rachel was growing up on a rural farm in Iowa, her parents were extremely strict. According to the Amish tradition, Rachel's parents were not allowed to use any kind of modern amenities, including the use of electricity or motorized vehicles.

Instead of using a tractor to plow the fields, Rachel's father would use an ox. If Rachel's family wanted to travel to town, they couldn't drive a car, they had to ride in a horse-drawn buggy. In the same way that Rachel's physical environment was strict and demanding, her emotional and spiritual upbringing was even worse. Although Rachel had been given a sweet, precious and loving heart by God, it didn't last very long because of all the authoritative rules and regulations she had to endure.

Rachel's childhood was similar to growing up in a home controlled by the Pharisees. Rachel's father was constantly angry and he would punish his children for the slightest mistake. In an attempt to protect his children from the seductive and alluring ways of the world, Rachel's father inflicted a lot of emotional abuse on his children in the form of excessive rules and regulations, and by doing so, he destroyed his precious daughter's heart.

Because Rachel was expected to get married between the ages of eighteen to twenty-five, she accepted the first wedding proposal that came her way. Although she desperately wanted to get out of her parent's house, Rachel found herself in the same situation many years later. Her loving husband, who used to be so sweet and kind, had turned into the same kind of man as her father. The harsh and demanding spirit of religion that had consumed her childhood was now being inflicted upon her own children.

When Rachel's eight-year-old son experienced an unfortunate accident that impaired his vision, it was too much to take. Rachel experienced an emotional breakdown and found herself locked up in a mental institution. She was unable to commune with her Heavenly Father like a trusting little child. She was living in constant fear of having committed the unforgivable sin of blasphemy against the Holy Spirit. Because Rachel's fear of being permanently separated from God for all eternity continued growing worse, she was no longer able to feel the loving presence of the Lord, even while praying or reading her Bible.

In order for Rachel to break free from the devil's bondage, she first needed to be convinced that God was not angry with her, and that she was not being punished. Rachel never committed an unforgivable sin, because the Holy Spirit was still actively involved in her life, trying to connect with her heart, the heart of a precious little child. The Holy Spirit wanted to take Rachel back into her past, so that Jesus could heal her childhood wounds and replace them with his incredible love.

Before Rachel could embark on the Lord's healing journey, she first needed to give God permission. After giving God permission, the next step Rachel needed to accomplish was to identify all the ways that she had been hurt. One challenge in Rachel's situation was the mental institution where she was staying had been giving her psychological medications designed to repress her negative emotions.

Because Rachel was able to cut back on her medications, she was able to connect with her heart and make a list of all the ways that she had been hurt during her childhood. This process took some time, because at first, Rachel didn't think there was anything wrong with her childhood. But after working with a Christian counselor for several weeks, Rachel was eventually able to break through her fears and identify some of the abuse that she had suffered.

After Rachel identified several events from her past where she had been hurt, the next step was to embrace the pain. To begin this process, Rachel used a meditative style of prayer where she invited Jesus to take her back in time to visit the hurt little girl from her childhood. The image that Rachel used looked similar to a scene from the television show *Little House on the Prairie*. In this meditative scene, there were rolling hills of amber grain, a simple farmhouse, and a hurt little girl working in the garden.

When Rachel invited Jesus into this scene, one of the Lord's top priorities was to minister to the hurt little girl in the garden. As Rachel approached the garden with the Lord by her side, she knew exactly why the little girl was crying. In an attempt to minister to the little girl, Rachel pictured herself picking up the child and holding her in her arms. The little girl had been hurt and needed love. Because Jesus has an endless supply of love, Rachel was able to interact with the child in such a way where the little girl could express all her hurt and fears, and in exchange, the Lord was able to replace all her hurt with an endless supply of his all-consuming love.

After Rachel was able to dig up all her repressed childhood hurt and replace that pain with the Lord's love, the next step was to forgive her father. Because

Rachel's father was a strict and harsh man, Rachel found it necessary to go back in time with Jesus to confront her father for all the times he failed to act in a godly manner. On one occasion, Rachel's father was yelling at the little girl for no reason. He was angry because he didn't have enough money to buy farming supplies and was taking his frustrations out on his children.

When Jesus approached the scene from the distance, Rachel's father immediately knew his actions were wrong. He fell to his knees and begged the Lord's forgiveness. As Jesus was ministering to this broken man, Rachel was able to pick up the little girl in her arms and explain to her father the proper way little girls needed to be loved. After explaining the proper way to treasure a little girl's precious heart, Rachel realized that her father didn't know any better—that he was only treating his children the same way that he had been treated.

After Rachel was able to embrace the hurt and pain from her past and forgive her father, her heart came alive. The Holy Spirit flooded her heart with love, peace and joy. Her God-given natural programming had been restored, and the devil's bondage was broken. Rachel was able to get off the doctor's psychological medication, leave the mental institution and return back home to her family.

In another situation, a man named Tony decided to look at pornography on the Internet even though he knew it was wrong. As soon as he did, a demonic spirit that had been assigned to his life gave him a hunger and thirst for more. All during this time, the Holy Spirit was screaming at Tony to stop, begging him to turn away from sexual immorality. Because Tony was enjoying his sin, he told the Holy Spirit, "No, I like how this makes me feel." As soon as Tony rejected the Holy Spirit's warning, demonic spirits attacked him even more, driving him deeper into bondage.

In the beginning stages of his addiction, Tony was satisfied with thirty minutes of entertainment per day, but then the demons wanted more. After a few months, Tony was driven to look at hard-core porn, and soon he began watching videos. Eventually the demons were able to influence Tony's thoughts to the point where he had crossed a physical barrier and started engaging in sexually immoral conversations. After establishing a few online friendships, he began having sex with prostitutes.

Tony was able to hide his sexual sins from his wife, Virginia, for about a year. Even though Virginia knew something was wrong, the demonic spirits that were operating in Tony's life would inspire him with clever ideas that he used as lies to hide his behaviors. All during this time, Tony continued to fall deeper into depression. He hated himself for being unfaithful to his wife, and the only way he could make himself feel better was turning back to his addiction. The more sex Tony had, the more he hated himself, and the more he hated himself, the more sex he needed to make himself feel better. It was a downward spiral of destruction.

Then one day Tony hit bottom and didn't want to live anymore. Instead of turning to a Christian counselor for help, Tony decided to tell Virginia everything. After explaining how a few dirty pictures on the Internet had grown into a lifestyle of sex with prostitutes, his wife was devastated. Virginia curled into a ball on the floor and cried for several hours. After a few days, Virginia packed up her personal belongings and left. She said to Tony, "I never want to see you again!"

With nowhere else to turn, Tony cried out to the God of his childhood. After repenting of his sins, the Holy Spirit welcomed him back and began working with him through the healing process. Because Tony wasn't born with a pornography addiction, the Holy Spirit needed to take Tony back into his childhood to show him the root cause of the problem. Even though Tony was able to understand the healing process in his mind, the actual healing and deliverance work needed to occur within his heart, the heart of a precious child.

When Tony was a little boy, he never received the love and support that he needed from his parents. His parents were constantly fighting and eventually their marriage ended in divorce. Because Tony was bounced back and forth between his mom's house and his father's apartment, he never felt loved. All of his hurt, rejection and abandoned feelings were repressed deep within his heart. Although Tony was born with the sweet, precious heart of a child, his repressed feelings of abandonment changed the way he viewed the world.

Even though Tony still had the ability to connect with his heart, he made a choice to live disconnected from his feelings, because they were too painful. In an attempt to avoid his pain, Tony did everything possible to live a life detached from his feelings. The only problem with living a life detached from his feelings was that God wanted to connect with Tony's heart. By avoiding his heart, Tony would also be avoiding a connection with God.

Another problem with living a life detached from his feelings was that demonic spirits could access Tony's repressed emotional wounds any time they wanted. For example, whenever demonic spirits wanted Tony to view more pornography on the Internet, all they needed to do was poke his childhood wounds, and instantly, Tony would experience the same rejection he did as a child. Upon experiencing those feelings, Tony had a choice to make: Would he turn to the Lord for healing, or would he turn back to his addiction in an attempt to make himself feel better?

The first step in Tony's healing process would be to acknowledge that God gave him a precious heart and that God wanted to commune with him deep in his heart. Because Tony had many years of repressed emotional pain in his heart, he would be required to embrace all that pain to see where it was coming from. Because Tony's pain was a direct result of his parents' neglect, Tony would be required to forgive his parents. Because the lack of forgiveness is a sin, that sin would give demonic spirits access to his life.

After Tony had identified all the times when he had felt rejected and abandoned as a child, the next step in his healing process was to invite Jesus back in time to visit the hurt little boy from his past. To accomplish this process, Tony used a meditative style of prayer. He imagined what it would be like if he could go back in time with Jesus and minister to the hurt little boy from his childhood.

In one scene, the room was totally dark. The little boy from his childhood was hiding under the bed. He didn't want to come out. When Tony entered the scene, he pulled back the curtains and opened up the windows. After flooding the room with light, and inviting Jesus into his bedroom, the light of Christ illuminated the darkness to the point where the little boy realized that no one was going to hurt him. Once the little boy felt safe, he came out from under the bed. As soon as he did, Tony was able to hold the child in his arms and assure him that he was loved.

Because Tony knew exactly what the little boy was feeling, he was able to speak to the child, giving him all the words of reassurance that he needed to hear. Tony spent hours holding the little boy in his arms, teaching him everything he needed to know to be a man after God's own heart. As Tony ministered to the little boy, Jesus was able to remove all his hurt and replace it with his all-consuming love.

After Tony had spent countless hours ministering to the little boy from his past, he felt the need to confront his parents. In one scene, his parents were angry and fighting. His mom was screaming at his father and threatening to leave because he had punched a hole in the wall. The little boy was traumatized and didn't want to see his family torn apart. When Tony entered the living room, he picked up the little boy and held him in his arms.

Because Tony invited Jesus into the scene, the presence of Christ began to soften everyone's hearts to the point where his parents knew that their actions were wrong. They felt terrible for the way they had been destroying their marriage and neglecting their precious child. After Tony explained to his parents the proper way for a husband to love his wife, and how a wife should love her husband, the entire family fell on their knees before the Lord, asking for his forgiveness.

After Tony embraced the pain of his past and forgave his parents, he felt ten pounds lighter. The devices the demons were using to drive his pornography addiction had been completely removed. Instead of turning to sex to make himself feel better, Tony could now commune with Jesus deep within his heart. After Tony had broken all the unhealthy soul-ties with the women he had sex with, he began praying for his wife.

Although Tony never expected to see his wife again, the Holy Spirit continued working in Virginia's life. During this time, many of Virginia's well-meaning friends were trying to persuade her to forgive her husband and move on with her life. Before Virginia could forgive her husband, she first needed to experience the fullness of her pain. She needed to embrace her pain, because it's not possible to go from a major loss directly to instant forgiveness without experiencing the painful grieving process in between.

In Virginia's situation, she needed many months to fully embrace her pain. During this time, the Lord held Virginia in his arms and let her cry as much as she needed. After Virginia had fully embraced her pain and grieved the loss of her marriage, the Lord started speaking to her about her need for forgiveness. One of the passages the Lord used to speak to Virginia was from Colossians 3:12–13, which says, *As God's chosen ones, holy and beloved, clothe yourselves with compassion, kindness, humility, meekness, and patience. Bear with one another and, if anyone has a complaint against another, forgive each other; just as the Lord has forgiven you, so you also must forgive.*

As soon as Virginia realized how many times she had betrayed the Lord's love, and how the Lord had forgiven her, she made a decision to truly forgive her husband. Once Virginia released Tony's entire debt to the Lord, she was able to exchange all her hurt and pain for God's all-consuming love. After several more months of hard work, the Lord was able to bring this couple back together. It took Virginia a very long time before she could fully trust her husband again, but with the Lord's assistance, Tony and Virginia's marriage has been fully restored.

USING A MEDITATIVE STYLE OF HEALING PRAYER

In the event that you have never experienced the fullness of God's incredible love, and are still holding onto some hurtful past events, you may want to spend some time communing with Jesus using a meditative style of healing prayer. To use a meditative style of prayer, all you need to do is find a quiet place in your home where you can be alone with the Lord for several hours.

1 The first step in this process would be to give Jesus permission to take you back into your past, so that he can bring up any negative events that need healing. You can begin this process with a simple prayer by saying, **Dear Lord Jesus, I give you permission to take me back into my past, to reveal any hurtful events, so that I can fully embrace the pain, forgive those who hurt me, and be set free—free to be the child of God that you have intended me to be.**

2 The next step would be to start your prayer by imagining a peaceful natural setting. For example, picture what it would be like to spend the day at the

beach with Jesus. Just close your eyes and picture a white sandy beach with a gentle tide. Imagine what it would be like to feel the sun on your face. After spending some time watching the seagulls hovering overhead, invite Jesus to join you in this setting. Picture what Jesus would look like. Allow yourself to fall into his loving arms.

3 After you spend some time expressing your love to Jesus, ask him to take you back into your past. Ask Jesus to bring up a hurtful past event that needs healing. Once a situation comes to mind, go back in time with Jesus and minister to that hurt little boy or girl who needs your love and support. Start by holding the child in your arms.

4 After you spend time allowing the little boy or girl to express all his or her feelings, ask Jesus to remove all of your negative emotions and replace them with his incredible love. In the event that you feel the need to confront the person who hurt you, ask Jesus to accompany you so that his love can soften that person's heart. After telling this person all the reasons why you have been hurt by his or her careless actions, find a way to grant that person forgiveness.

5 After you allow Jesus to minister to all the parties involved, ask the little boy or girl from your past if he or she would like to go someplace fun and spend time with Jesus. If the little boy or girl would like to visit a beach, imagine what it would be like to watch that child playing with Jesus in the sand. After engaging in some fun time, tell the precious child just how much you love him or her, and then close your prayer by leaving your beloved childhood friend with Jesus.

Another option for experiencing God's incredible love through the forgiveness process would be to write several healing letters. After you identify ten of the worst events that you have experienced in the past, set a goal to write one healing letter per day, for the next ten days.

THE EMOTIONAL HEALING LETTER EXERCISE

1 Spend some time in prayer and ask the Lord to bring up ten unresolved emotional issues. If the Lord brings to mind some people who have hurt you, ask the Holy Spirit to bring back the fullness of your repressed emotions, so that you can be set free.

2 After you identify ten hurtful past events that need healing, try to separate those situations from everything else that has happened to you. Instead of trying to work through years of emotional abuse at one time, try to isolate one experience, and keep working on that situation until it is resolved.

3 Begin the exercise from a prayerful and meditative state of mind. Find a quiet place where you can be alone with the Lord. Make sure you have plenty of tissues and the necessary writing supplies.

4 Picture the person who hurt you in your imagination. Imagine that person can hear everything you are about to say. If the person is deceased, picture them in heaven standing next to Jesus.

5 Begin writing your letter with the words, *I'm angry because you hurt me!* Tell this person all the ways that he or she has hurt you by his or her careless and

disrespectful actions. Keep writing the words *I'm angry*, over and over again. Release all your anger on paper. Don't worry about spelling or grammar; just release everything that needs to be said.

6 After you release all your anger, move on to any fears that you may have experienced. How has this person affected your life? Describe how the consequences of his or her careless actions have carried forward into your present-day relationships.

7 After you release any fears or guilty feelings, get in touch with your sadness. Tell this person what you wanted to happen that didn't. If you're writing to your father say, *I'm sad because I wanted a better relationship with you. I wanted you to treat me like a beloved son or daughter. I wanted your love and support.*

8 Conclude your letter with anything else you need to say to this person, and then begin a new letter by picturing the person who hurt you in a completely healed state. Picture them in heaven standing next to Jesus. Imagine this person full of God's love, and because they are full of God's love, allow them to offer you an apology.

9 Start your apology letter by saying, *I'm sorry for hurting you. You didn't deserve to be treated like that. I'm so sorry. Please forgive me.* Write down all the loving words that you need to hear.

10 Conclude your apology letter with prayer. Release the person who hurt you into the Lord's hands. Ask Jesus to wash away any negativity that you may have picked up by accepting this person's abuse. Surrender this person to the Lord, and if appropriate, ask Jesus to break all unhealthy soul-ties.

11 Allow Jesus to speak to you through a closure letter. Accept the Lord's love and forgiveness. Allow the Lord's love and forgiveness to flow into your heart and cleanse you of all curses, resentment and negativity.

12 Ask the Lord to show you if there's anything else that you need to release. Allow yourself to fall into the Lord's arms and be permanently set free—free to be the child of God the Lord intended you to be.

RENOUNCING LODGES & SECRET SOCIETIES

Although many lodges and secret societies may appear to be a loyal gathering of men who meet together on a regular basis for the purpose of conducting charity, if that were the case, there wouldn't be any reason for the members to make secret vows. If these men were performing authentic works of charity, they would want the entire world to see their good deeds, but as it is, many of these organizations use secret vows to conceal their demonic activities.

A good example of the demonic activities that occur within secret societies comes from a member initiation ceremony that was performed inside of a Masonic temple.[1] In one ceremony, several new members were blindfolded and made to kneel on the ground before the Great Architect of the Universe. As these men were kneeling, the Worshipful Master took turns placing a sword upon each of the men's chests. The men were asked to touch the object and describe what it felt like.

After all the men described a sharp metal sword, they were asked to swear an oath to never tell anyone what happened to them during the darkness of the rituals and to honor whatever they saw in the light. After all the men took turns swearing an oath, the Worshipful Master holding the sword said, "The meaning of the sword that touched your chest is that if you do not keep your promise, you will regret it and suffer from it the rest of your life."

After these men were subjected to other forms of intimidation by having a noose placed around their necks, the Worshipful Master said, "Bring the candidates forward that are searching for the true light." (If these men were authentic Christians, they wouldn't be searching for the true light, they would already know Jesus as *the light of the world.*[2])

After the men were taken into an inner chamber, they repeated another vow before the Great Architect of the Universe by saying, "I swear with all my strength, with all my will, and with full sincerity, not to disclose any Masonic secrets, and to work toward the common good and goals of the Masons." (When these men acknowledged the Great Architect of the Universe as their god, they would be making agreements with demonic spirits. If these men were authentic Christians, they would be working to advance God's kingdom, not the Mason's agenda.)

After all the men repeated this vow, they were asked to drink wine out of a human skull while swearing another oath by saying, "May this wine I now drink become a deadly poison to me should I ever knowingly or willfully disclose any of the Masonic secrets."

After these men had completed their initiation ceremony, they were expected to attend regular meetings at the lodge where they would conduct more satanic rituals. For example, a few days before Easter, these men would gather for a demonic communion service. During this service, the Worshipful Master would say,

"We meet this day to commemorate the death of our most wise and perfect master, not as inspired or divine, for that is not for us to decide, but as of least, the greatest of the apostles of mankind."[3]

In this statement, the men would be denying the deity of Christ. Jesus is either the second person of the Blessed Trinity, the divine manifestation of God in the flesh, or he was just an ordinary man. By participating in this ritual, these men would be saying that it was *not* their responsibility to decide whether Jesus was the Son of God or if he was just a great human leader.

After these men denied the deity of Christ, they mocked the death of Jesus on the cross by saying, "It's too bad that the leader of the Apostles is now dead and gone forever." By making these kinds of statements, the men would be denying the redemptive work of Christ on the cross, and in doing so, they would be rejecting the Lord's sacrifice on the cross for the forgiveness of their sins. (Jesus is either the Sacrificial Lamb of God who paid the penalty for our sins, or he was just some unfortunate carpenter who was crucified with several other criminals.) After these men denied the deity of Christ, they would receive a false form of communion.

In order for these men to move higher into the ranks of Freemasonry, they had to perform deeper, darker and more satanic rituals. Because Freemasonry has thirty-three degrees, the men at the top levels are required to perform blood sacrifices. For example, in one high-level ritual, the members had gathered around a pentagram drawn on the floor and were drinking the blood of a goat that had been sacrificed to Satan.

Because of the satanic nature of these rituals, the Congregation for the Doctrine of the Faith has issued many warnings over the years forbidding the faithful from participating in Freemasonry. In a document entitled *Irreconcilability Between Christian Faith and Freemasonry*, the Catholic Church *affirms that membership in Masonic associations remains forbidden by the Church, and the faithful who enrolls in them are in a state of grave sin and may not receive Holy Communion.*[4]

Because most lodges and secret societies are nothing more than a gateway to the occult, you may want to review the following list of names to see if there are any organizations that you have been involved with in the past: Freemasonry, the Order of Amaranth, Oddfellows, Buffalos, Druids and Foresters Lodges, the Ku Klux Klan, The Grange, the Woodmen of the World, Riders of the Red Robe, the Knights of Pythias, the Mystic Order of the Veiled Prophets of the Enchanted Realm, the women's Orders of the Eastern Star and of the White Shrine of Jerusalem, the Daughters of the Eastern Star, the International Orders of Job's Daughters, the Rainbow Girls and the boys' Order of De Molay.

In the event that you have made secret vows or participated in demonic rituals through any of these lodges or secret societies, you can use the following prayer to break those agreements in the name, power and authority of Jesus.

Lord Jesus, I come to you as a sinner seeking forgiveness and healing from all sins committed against you by my family lineage. I honor my earthly father, mother and ancestors, but I utterly turn away from and renounce all their sins, especially those that have exposed me to any kind of harmful influence. I forgive all my ancestors for the effects of their sins, and I ask to be washed clean of their destructive consequences.

I renounce and rebuke Satan and every evil power that has affected my family lineage. I renounce and forsake my involvement in all lodges, secret societies and any other evil craft practiced by my ancestors. I renounce all oaths and rituals in every level and degree. I renounce witchcraft, the spirit of the antichrist and the curse of any demonic doctrine. I renounce idolatry, blasphemy and all destructive forms of secrecy and deception. I renounce the love of power, the love of money, and any fears that have held me in bondage.

I renounce all spiritually binding oaths taken in Freemasonry, Mormonism, the Order of Amaranth, Oddfellows, Buffalos, Druids and Foresters Lodges, the Ku Klux Klan, The Grange, the Woodmen of the World, Riders of the Red Robe, the Knights of Pythias, the Mystic Order of the Veiled Prophets of the Enchanted Realm, the women's Orders of the Eastern Star and of the White Shrine of Jerusalem, the Daughters of the Eastern Star, the International Orders of Job's Daughters, the Rainbow Girls and the boys' Order of De Molay, and any other secret society, along with their destructive effects on me and my family.

I renounce the blindfold and hoodwink, and any effects they had on my emotions and eyes, including all confusion and fears. I renounce the noose around the neck, the fear of choking and any spirit that causes difficulty in breathing. I renounce the effects of all pagan objects and symbolism, aprons, books of rituals, rings and jewelry. I renounce the entrapping of others and observing the helplessness of others during rituals. I renounce false communion, all mockery of the redemptive work of Jesus Christ on the cross, all unbelief, confusion and deception, and all worship of Lucifer as a god.

I humbly ask for your forgiveness, Lord Jesus, and for your blood to cleanse me of all the sins I have committed. Please purify my spirit, soul, mind, emotions and every other part of my body. Please destroy any evil spirits that have attached themselves to me, or my family, because of these sins and cleanse us with the fire of your Holy Spirit. I invite you into my heart, Lord Jesus, and enthrone you as my Lord and Savior for all eternity.

DENOUNCING CULTS THAT DENY THE TRINITY

Another doorway the devil uses to ensnare souls comes from religious cults that deny the divinity of Christ. A good example of a religious cult that uses secret vows and temple rituals comes from the Church of Jesus Christ of Latter Day Saints, more commonly known as the Mormon Church.

The Mormon Church was established by Joseph Smith in 1830 after he claimed to have received a vision from God. As a young man, Joseph used to practice witchcraft by using a seer stone to help his father in a business they called *money digging*. In an effort to discover the location of buried treasure, Joseph would place the seer stone inside of his hat and pull the hat up to his face to block out all the sunlight. Because the seer stone was charged with supernatural powers, it allowed Joseph to gaze into the spiritual realm where he could observe spirits that were guarding the buried treasure.

Once Joseph received this information, he would guide his father to the exact location of where to dig. In addition to using a seer stone, Joseph Smith also wore a Jupiter talisman around his neck that he considered to be his most valuable possession. One day while Joseph was invoking supernatural powers from his Jupiter talisman, an angel named Moroni told him about a secret manuscript written on golden plates that contained the true gospel of god. After making this discovery, Joseph translated that information into the *Book of Mormon.*[1]

During this time, Joseph was also involved in Freemasonry where he quickly rose through the ranks to the highest level. Because Joseph was very familiar with Freemasonry, he was able to incorporate many of the rituals from the Masonic temple into the Mormon temple. He also incorporated many practices from the Masonic temple into the *Book of Mormon.* For example, when writing the *Book of Mormon,* he used terms such as *ancient orders, degrees, candidates, secrets, lodges, keys, tokens* and the *order of the priesthood.*

Because the *Book of Mormon* was inspired from Joseph's involvement with Freemasonry, and directly influenced through his occult practices of divination and spirit guide channeling, the Mormon Church believes that there are millions of gods in our galaxy, and each god rules over his own planet. They also believe that when the god for the planet Earth was a little boy, he sought after holiness, and after his efforts were rewarded, he was exalted to godhood where he joined millions of other gods in our universe.[2]

The Mormon Church also believes that the god for the planet Earth lives with our heavenly mother, having celestial sex in an attempt to produce billions of spirit babies. The salvation plan for the planet Earth was established when the two oldest spirit babies (Jesus and Lucifer) started fighting over the best way to rule the planet. Because Lucifer wanted to rule the planet by force, while Jesus wanted to allow the human race to experience their own free will, it was decided that Jesus had a better salvation plan, so Lucifer staged a rebellion, and was banished to Earth along with his followers.

The Mormon Church also believes that Jesus was married to at least three wives including Mary, Martha and Mary Magdalene. They also believe that Jesus had many children and that Joseph Smith is a direct descendant of Jesus' lineage. Mormons also believe that if they strive after holiness, and follow all the rules of the Mormon Church, that they too can become gods and rule over their own planet someday.[3]

In order for church members to rule over their own planet, they need to pass through two temple rituals called the *endowment ceremony* and the *sealing right*. In one ceremony, the participants dressed in long white robes and were asked to take a vow by a high priest who said, "Do you promise to accept the law of consecration, and do you consecrate yourself today, your time and talent, to the Church of Jesus Christ of Latter Day Saints for the establishment of Zion?"[4]

After the participants entered into this spiritually binding agreement, the high priest said, "I seal upon you all the blessings of kingdoms, thrones, principalities, powers, dominions and exaltations."[5] (Although many of these attributes are used to describe the ranks of good and holy angels, they are also used to describe the ranks of fallen angels. In the event that demonic spirits have been given permission to operate inside of Mormon temples, the participants who enter into this vow would be receiving spiritual powers from demonic kingdoms, thrones and principalities.)

After the candidates completed their initiation ceremony, they were allowed to enter the temple and perform more rituals. Because Mormons believe that their religion is the only true religion, and that a person needs to perform all the temple rituals in order to become a god and rule over his or her own planet, some of the church members were concerned about the people who were born hundreds of years before the Mormon temples were built. (The first Mormon temple was constructed in Kirtland, Ohio in 1836.)

In an effort to address this concern, the Mormon Church has acquired a huge database of genealogy records so that they can perform *baptisms for the dead*. During this ritual, members dress in white robes and are submerged in a baptismal font. As a person is being submerged, a temple worker will say, "Sister Johnston, having been commissioned of Jesus Christ, I baptize you on behalf of Marianne Johnston, who is now dead." After Sister Johnston has been submerged in water, the temple worker will repeat this process for all her deceased relatives in an attempt to impart supernatural powers into her entire family lineage.

In another ritual, the participants needed to pass through a veil before they could enter the most holy inner sanctuary called the *celestial room*. After approaching the veil, a temple worker would extend his hand through an opening in the veil to give the person who wanted to enter a special handshake. For example, the temple worker would take his right index finger and press it into the sensitive area of the other person's wrist and say, "What is that?"[6]

The person who wanted to enter the celestial room would respond by saying, "The first token of the priesthood."

Then the temple worker said, "Has it a name?"

The other person responded by saying, "It has."

Then the temple worker said, "Will you give it to me?"

The person responded by saying, "I will through the veil."

This process went on for several minutes until the person verified all the special handshakes and secret code words. Once inside the celestial room, church members can then participate in the *true order of prayer.*

Members who participate in the temple rituals must also wear sacred undergarments at all times. These undergarments are marked with Masonic symbols that impart the "supernatural powers of the priesthood." For example, the *mark of the square* is located on a person's right breast and "suggests to the mind exactness and honor." The *mark of the compass* is located on a person's left breast and "suggests to the mind an undeviating course leading to eternal life."[7]

One of the major theological problems that Satan uses to ensnare souls in the Mormon religion is a belief that denies the divinity of Christ. For example, if a Mormon missionary knocked on your door, and you asked that person if he prayed directly to Jesus as God, he would probably respond by saying, "We pray in Jesus' name." If you continued asking the same question, "Do you pray directly to Jesus as God?" the missionary would probably say, "We believe in Jesus of the Bible, and we pray in Jesus' name."

The reason that Mormons don't pray directly to Jesus, or worship Jesus as the second person of the

Trinity, is that they don't believe that Jesus is the divine manifestation of God in the flesh. They believe that Jesus was just another one of Elohim's spirit babies (the same as Lucifer) and if they follow all the rules and regulations of the Mormon Church, they will become gods themselves and rule over their own planet. Because spirit babies don't pray to other spirit babies, Mormons would never pray directly to Jesus.

The problem with rejecting Jesus as the second person of the Trinity is that a person would also be rejecting the Gospel message at the same time. Because God has declared the penalty for sin to be death, there are only two options for sinners: We can either allow Jesus to pay the death penalty on our behalf, or we can pay the death penalty ourselves. By rejecting the Lord's sacrifice on the cross for the forgiveness of our sins, a person would also be rejecting God's plan of salvation. By rejecting God's plan for salvation, that person would run the risk of being eternally separated from God for all eternity.

OTHER CULTS THAT DENY THE DIVINITY OF CHRIST

The same problem of rejecting the divinity of Christ also exists within the Jehovah's Witnesses. According to Watchtower publications, Jehovah's Witnesses believe that Jesus is a spirit creature, similar to a super angel. After God created the lower-ranking angels, he created the world and sent one of his super angels to Earth to be born of the Virgin Mary and named him Jesus.[8]

Jehovah's Witnesses do *not* believe that Jesus died on the Cross of Calvary for the forgiveness of sins, but rather on a large stake. After his death, the Lord's body was laid in a tomb where it was completely disintegrated by God. When Jesus appeared to his disciples after his death, God rematerialized this angelic being into different bodies to provide proof of his resurrection. When this spiritual being returns during the battle of Armageddon, he will destroy everybody except for Jehovah's Witness church members. This spiritual being will always remain invisible to everybody except for 144,000 select Jehovah's Witnesses, who will rule with him from heaven for all eternity.

Jehovah's Witnesses also enforce other cult-like doctrines that prevent their church members from associating with any ex-members of their religion. In the event that one of their church members is excommunicated, or leaves the church on his or her own accord, the rest of the members consider that person to be a follower of Satan. Jehovah's Witnesses also view other Christian denominations as pagan, demonic enemies of God. They also believe that Satan controls all born-again Christians.[9]

In an attempt to eliminate all the places in Scripture that speak of the divinity of Christ, Jehovah's Witnesses have produced their own version of the Bible called the *New World Translation of the Holy Scriptures*. In this version, many passages have been changed to impart a slightly different meaning. For example, John 1:1–3 says, *In the beginning was the Word, and the Word was with God, and the Word was God. He was in the beginning with God. All things came into being through him, and without him not one thing came into being.* Because Jehovah's Witnesses would never agree with this statement, they changed the text in their version of the Bible so that it says, "In the beginning was the Word, and the Word was with God, and the Word was a god."[10]

Jehovah's Witnesses also had a problem with the Book of Hebrews because it contains several Old Testament references that prove Christ's superiority to the angels. For example, Hebrews 1:5–6 says, *For to which of the angels did God ever say, "You are my Son; today I have begotten you"? Or again, "I will be his Father, and he will be my Son"? And again, when he brings the firstborn into the world, he says, "Let all God's angels worship him."* Because an angelic being would never worship another angelic being, Jehovah's Witnesses had to change the meaning of Sacred Scripture to make their version of the Bible line up with their theology.

The problem with denying the divinity of Christ is that it prevents a person from entering into an authentic relationship with the Blessed Trinity. If Jesus is nothing more that a mortal man, then no one would spend their time praying to him. If Jesus is nothing more than an angelic being, then no one would worship him as God. If Jesus is not the Good Shepherd who leads and guides his sheep, then no one would spend their time resting in the Sacred Silence, in an attempt to hear his voice.

If Jesus is not the Lamb of God who paid the death penalty on our behalf, then no one would accept the Gospel message. When people fail to accept the Gospel message, they run the risk of being eternally separated from God for all eternity. If Jesus is not the divine manifestation of God in the flesh, then no one is going to apply his teaching to his or her life. In the event that a person fails to make Jesus the Lord of his or her life, then that person may hear the Lord say on the last day, *"I never knew you; go away from me, you evildoers."*[11]

In the event that you have participated in a religious cult that controls its members through fear, false doctrine and intimidation, or have made numerous vows and agreements while performing rituals inside a demonic temple, it may take some time to break free from Satan's bondage. One way to begin this process would be to study the *Catechism of the Catholic Church.*

Many of the heresies that exist in today's religious cults have already been refuted hundreds of years ago during the Councils of Constantinople, Florence and Toledo. According to the Catechism in section 266, *We worship one God in the Trinity and the Trinity in unity, without either confusing the persons or dividing the substance; for the person of the Father is one, the Son's is another, the Holy Spirit's another; but the Godhead of the Father, Son and Holy Spirit is one, their glory equal, their majesty coeternal.*[12]

Another powerful passage that you may want to apply to your life comes from section 260 of the Catechism that says, *The ultimate end of the whole divine economy is the entry of God's creatures into the perfect unity of the Blessed Trinity.*[13]

After you have spent some time studying the Catechism, and have denounced all the devil's lies concerning the divinity of Christ, it would be helpful to search your past to identify any vows and agreements that you have made while participating in cults, along with any rituals that you have performed inside of pagan shrines or demonic temples. After you make a list of all these vows, agreements and rituals, you can break them in the name, power and authority of Jesus.

Other forms of devil worship and religious cults that deny the divinity of Christ would include:

Black Mass — A satanic ritual performed to mock the Catholic Mass. In a black mass, the Lord's Prayer is recited backward, communion is desecrated and animals are sacrificed. Other rituals include sexual orgies and vows to Satan so that the participants can acquire more demonic powers.

Christian Science — Is a series of metaphysical beliefs and practices from the Church of Christ Scientist that was founded in 1879. Members believe that only God and the mind have ultimate reality, and that sin and illness are illusions of nonexistent matter that can be overcome by positive thinking. The founder taught that Jesus is *not* God, but rather a *divine nature* that's available to all mankind to overcome sickness and death.

New Age Movement — Is a broad spectrum of spirituality characterized by a group of individual seekers, healers and teachers. Rather than following any organized religion, New Age practitioners typically construct their own forms of spirituality using aspects from Eastern religions, Wicca, past-life experiences, spirit guide channeling and other occult practices.

Santeria — A religion based on Yoruba beliefs and traditions that spread to the Caribbean islands by African slaves. Because the African slaves were forced to convert to Catholicism, they associated their African gods (called orishas) with a corresponding Catholic saint. That way, the slaves could continue worshiping their African gods, while at the same time pleasing their owners. Oftentimes Santeria rituals involve dancing, the casting of spells and animal sacrifices.

Scientology — Is a religion founded in 1952 by a science fiction writer who believes that every person is an immortal spiritual being that is trapped inside of his or her own body, and that every person has had multiple bodies over many lifetimes. Because every person has collected many traumas in each lifetime, the way to get rid of these traumas is through a process called *auditing* that helps people become more self-aware. It is through the process of becoming more self-aware that a person can achieve a god-like status.

Spiritualist Churches — Are a group of independent organizations that do not adhere to a single creed but believe the dead are able to communicate with the living with the assistance of a spirit medium. Mediums develop their abilities by participating in development circles with other psychics. The leaders of these churches use a combination of metaphysical, Buddhist and Hindu practices to connect with those who have died in an attempt to receive information from the spirit realm.

Unification Churches — A religious movement founded in South Korea in 1954. The founder's worldview included a combination of Eastern philosophy, Taoism and occultism along with a distorted interpretation of the Bible. The founder was also a medium who frequently communicated with the spirit realm and urged his followers to engage in spirit guide channeling for their own personal growth.

Voodoo Ceremonies — A form of witchcraft that started in Benin and spread throughout the world to nations such as Haiti. Voodoo practitioners invite Loa spirits into themselves during the ceremonies. They also sacrifice animals, cast spells and practice divination.

Wicca — A form of witchcraft that worships a mother goddess and her companion called *the horned god,* which they believe is in everything, including rocks, trees, earth and sky. Many Wiccans will cast spells in an attempt to influence the forces of earth, wind, fire and water. Wiccans will also incorporate aspects of astrology, divination and white magic into their spells in an attempt to manipulate the forces of nature to provide them with whatever they want. Because the Wiccan religion doesn't have any centralized beliefs, many Wiccans live by a code that says, *harm no one, do what you will,* which allows them to do almost anything they want.

DEVELOPING A DEEPER RELATIONSHIP WITH GOD

One day when Jesus was proclaiming the good news about the kingdom of heaven, he noticed a young man who couldn't speak. After calling the lad forward, he commanded a demonic spirit to come out of him, and *when the demon had gone out, the one who had been mute spoke, and the crowds were amazed.*[1]

After Jesus cast the demonic spirit out of the young man, he presented a very important teaching on spiritual warfare by saying, *"When the unclean spirit has gone out of a person, it wanders through waterless regions looking for a resting place, but not finding any, it says, 'I will return to my house from which I came.' When it comes, it finds it swept and put in order. Then it goes and brings seven other spirits more evil than itself, and they enter and live there; and the last state of that person is worse than the first."*[2]

After the demonic spirit had been cast out of the young man's life, it wandered through the *waterless regions looking for a resting place,*[3] and when the demon couldn't find another victim, it returned to the young man in an attempt to gain access to his life. In the event that the young man failed to fill his spiritual house with the power and presence of God, the demonic spirit would have brought back seven more evil spirits to gain access. If the young man failed to defend the spiritual integrity of his house, the demons would have been able to overpower him, *and the last state of that person would have been worse than the first.*[4]

Another option for the young man in this situation would be to fill his spiritual house with the power and presence of God. That way, he would have been able to defend the spiritual integrity of his house, so that he would *not* fall back into bondage. In the event that the young man accepted the Gospel message, when the demonic spirits returned, they would have found his spiritual house fully occupied with the Lord Jesus Christ. If that were the case, there may have been a major spiritual battle, but if the young man was serious about growing in holiness and obedience to the Lord, the devil and his vast army of fallen angels could not touch him.

In the same way, if you have experienced a recent liberation from evil spirits by denouncing any New Age or occult activities, or by breaking any unhealthy vows or sexual soul-ties, it may be helpful to prepare yourself for a serious spiritual battle. Once a person leaves the kingdom of darkness and enters the kingdom of light, the devil will do everything in his power to allure and seduce that person back into bondage, using the same tactics and temptations that have always worked in the past.

Because the devil is unwilling to let people leave his domain without first testing their resolve, it would be helpful to make sure your spiritual house is fully occupied with the power and presence of Christ. The first step in this process would be to understand and accept the Gospel message.

UNDERSTANDING AND ACCEPTING THE GOSPEL MESSAGE

The first requirement for a person to transition out of the kingdom of darkness and into the marvelous light would be to understand and accept the Gospel message. The Gospel message is a legal contract between you and God that has been described in the Catechism under sections 599–682. It works similar to a binding legal contract that moves a person out of Satan's kingdom and into God's kingdom.

Before you can enter this contract, you will first need to understand how it works, and know what it means, but unfortunately, very few people are able to describe the Good News, much less deliver the Gospel message to others. In the event that you think you know how to deliver the Gospel message, you can take the self-test right now. Go ahead and try to present the Gospel message to one of your friends or neighbors. What would you say to a person who doesn't have any religious background?

If God were calling you to deliver the Gospel message to a group of villagers in Malaysia, Mongolia or Madagascar, how would you prepare your message? If you think you have the answer, it may be helpful to set up an imaginary audience in your home. Picture a group of villagers seated in your living room, and then start preaching to them. See if you can preach for ten minutes by describing how a person can have his or her sins forgiven. How does a person enter into an authentic relationship with Jesus?

One way to deliver the Gospel message would be to acknowledge that all men and women are sinners. Because sin separates humanity from God, and all sin leads to death, God has issued a death penalty for all sinners. Because all men and women are sinners, every person has a choice to make: We can allow Jesus to pay the death penalty on our behalf, or we can pay the death penalty ourselves.

A longer version of the Gospel message begins with Romans 6:23, where God says, *"The wages of sin is death."* In the Old Covenant, when a man sinned he was allowed to place the penalty upon an innocent lamb. The lamb was slaughtered in the temple, and the lamb's blood atoned for the man's sin.

In the New Covenant, Jesus became the Lamb of God. Although Jesus lived a sinless life, he was condemned to die a violent death on the cross to make atonement for our sins. He was crucified, died and rose from the dead three days later. Now that Jesus has become the sacrificial Lamb of God, everybody still has a choice to make: You can pay the death penalty yourself, or you can allow Jesus to pay the penalty on your behalf.

To explore this meaning further, it may be helpful to imagine what it would be like to stand in front of God's throne on the Day of Judgment. Picture what it would look like if all your sins were piled high upon your head—all the people you hurt and all your disobedient acts. Because God is perfectly holy, no form of sin, darkness or deception can ever enter his eternal presence. Although God is loving and doesn't want to see any of his children suffer, he is also a God of justice.

When we sin, our actions harm other people. Because God loves the people whom our sins have harmed, he cannot simply turn his back on them and pretend they don't exist.

As you picture yourself standing in the heavenly courtroom awaiting judgment, ponder for a moment God's dilemma. Your sins, no matter how small, have harmed other people. All sin is an agreement with evil. Because you have sinned and fallen short of God's perfect standard of perfection, God needs to render a just verdict.

The very same people you have harmed may also be standing in the courtroom during your judgment. God cannot simply say, "Even though you hurt all these people, I'm going to ignore their pain and suffering." Such a statement may affirm God's love for you, but it would be in direct conflict with his perfectly holy and just nature.

It is for this reason that the penalty for sin is death. All have sinned and fallen short of God's standard of perfection, and now someone needs to pay the price. After God examines the evidence, he issues a guilty verdict and requires the penalty to be paid in full.

Picture what it would be like to be escorted to a holding cell to await your execution. Picture what it would be like to pay the death penalty for your sinful actions. The bars inside the jail cell are made of solid steel, the concrete walls are cold and dark, and there's no window or hope of escape.

Now picture Jesus the Messiah entering your cell dressed in sparkling white clothes. As you look into his eyes, it's apparent that he loves you very much. He reaches out his hand to take hold of your hand. He sits down next to you. Speaking in a soft voice, he draws near and says, "I will pay the penalty on your behalf. You can now go free."

Do you want to accept the Lord's offer? Will you allow Jesus to pay the death penalty on your behalf?

To accept the Lord's sacrifice, all you need to do is say a simple prayer from the sincerity of a contrite heart. Dear Lord Jesus, I come before you sinful. My actions have harmed other people, and I'm truly sorry. Please forgive me. I realize that the penalty for sin is death, and I don't want to pay the penalty myself. I accept your sacrifice on the cross for the forgiveness of my sins. I place all my sinful actions upon your cross and ask to be washed clean. Please transform my life through the power of your Holy Spirit. I surrender my life into your service. Please help me to become the child of God that you have intended me to be.

After you have accepted the Lord's sacrifice on the cross for the forgiveness of your sins, you now have direct access to God's throne room. You can enter the heavenly court anytime you want and speak directly to your Heavenly Father through prayer. You will be able to ask God questions, and after resting in the Sacred Silence and meditating on his will, you will be able to discern the Lord's will for your life.

ACCOMPLISHING GOD'S WILL IN YOUR LIFE

In order to accomplish God's will in your life, it will be necessary to surrender your life into the Lord's service. All you need to say to God is, I will do whatever you want from here on out. The problem with making this statement is that most people want to be their own god. Most people would rather make decisions in life based on their own personal pleasure, comfort and popularity, rather than on what's in their soul's best interest for all eternity.

Once you make a commitment to serve the Lord, the next step would be to pray and listen for your first assignment. This process is called *contemplative prayer*, and it's described in the Catechism under sections 2709–2719. To begin this process, all you need to do is find a quiet place in your home. You may find it helpful to begin your prayer by closing your eyes and picturing a peaceful, natural setting. Maybe you could envision a beautiful meadow with tall green grass, colorful wild-flowers and a flowing stream.

After you invite Jesus to join you in the natural set-ting, picturing what he would look like. Is he happy to see you? Can you express your love for him? Try saying the words out loud, "I love you, Jesus." After express-ing your love verbally, try communicating with Jesus using the silent language of your heart. After engaging your heart in prayer, allow yourself to feel your love for Jesus, and then direct that love to him. Other options would include falling into the Lord's loving arms and resting in the Sacred Silence.

After you are able to establish a Spirit-filled connection with Jesus, you can begin asking the Lord questions about your life. You may want to reconfirm your desire to serve the Lord by praying, Dear Lord Jesus, I surrender my life into your service. I will do whatever you want from here on out. I am your servant and you are my Master. What do you want me to do next? What changes do you want me to make in my life?

After you ask the Lord questions about your life, you will need to sit in silence and discern the Lord's answers. The Lord will speak to everybody differently. All you need to do is develop your own personal prayer language with Jesus. By engaging your heart in this process, the Lord will speak to you in a way that you will know what he wants you to do next.

After you receive your first assignment, you will need to proceed in obedience. If the Lord is calling you to remove worldly activities from your life, you will need to be obedient. Instead of spending countless hours watching television shows and worldly movies, you could spend that time in prayer.

If the Lord places a vision on your heart about orphaned children living in the trash dump, you could begin the discernment process by asking Jesus more questions. For example, you could pray, Dear Lord Jesus, do you want me to go on a mission trip? Yes or no? If you feel an affirmative response, the next question to ask would be, where and when?

By asking the Lord specific questions about your life and discerning his answers, you will be developing an authentic relationship with Jesus. If Jesus is calling you on a mission trip to proclaim the Gospel message to villagers, then the Holy Spirit will accompany you on your journey. If the Holy Spirit accompanies you, your heart will be filled with great joy as you work in partnership with God, accomplishing the Father's will for your life.

Then on the last day, you will have the opportunity to hear the Lord say, *"Well done, good and trustworthy slave; you have been trustworthy in a few things, I will put you in charge of many things; enter into the joy of your master."*[5]

NOTES

An Introduction to the Enemy
1. Revelation 12:7–9 & 12.
2. Genesis 3:1.
3. Genesis 3:2–3.
4. Genesis 3:4–5.
5. Genesis 3:6.
6. Ibid.
7. Genesis 3:7.
8. Genesis 3:8–9.
9. Genesis 3:10.
10. Genesis 3:11.
11. Genesis 3:12–13.
12. Genesis 3:22–24.
13. Genesis 6:5–6.
14. Genesis 3:6.

The Mechanics of Spiritual Warfare
1. Acts 19:11–17.
2. Acts 19:16.
3. Mark 16:15–18.
4. Father Gabriele Amorth, *An Exorcist Tells His Story* (San Francisco, CA: Ignatius Press, 1999), p. 153.
5. *The Roman Ritual: Christian Burial, Exorcism and Reserved Blessings* (Milwaukee WI: The Bruce Publishing Company, 1952), p. 187.

Communicating with Demonic Spirits
1. 1 Samuel 28:5.
2. 1 Samuel 28:6.
3. 1 Samuel 28:7–9.
4. 1 Samuel 28:10–11.
5. 1 Samuel 28:12–17 & 28:19–20.
6. 1 Samuel 28:15.
7. John 10:10.

Denouncing the Sin of Divination
1. Acts 16:16.
2. Ibid.
3. Acts 16:19 & 22.

Talismans, Amulets & Good Luck Charms
1. John 10:10.

Alcohol, Marijuana & Pharmaceutical Drugs
1. Mark 5:3–4.

Breaking Sinful Agreements with Evil
1. Catechism of the Catholic Church: 1451, Council of Trent (1551): DS 1676 & p. 872.
2. Catechism of the Catholic Church: 1459.

Sexual Immorality & Unhealthy Soul-Ties
1. John 10:10.
2. Rachel's Vineyard Ministries, "Abortions Impact: How Abortion Affected Me." Accessed July 10, 2017: http://www.rachelsvineyard.org/emotions/affects.aspx.
3. Project Rachel Ministry, "Adverse Psychological Reactions: A Fact Sheet." Accessed July 10, 2017: http://hopeafterabortion.com/?page_id=213#Literature.
4. Rachel's Vineyard Ministries, "Symptoms of Post-Abortion Trauma." Accessed July 10, 2017: http://www.rachelsvineyard.org/emotions/symptoms.aspx.
5. *New Webster's Dictionary and Thesaurus of the English Language* (Danbury, CT: Lexicon Publications Inc., 1992), p. 369.
6. 1 Corinthians 6:13 & 15–18.
7. John 8:9–11.

Avoiding Unhealthy Relationships
1. 2 Corinthians 6:14–18.

Taking Negative Thoughts Captive
1. 2 Corinthians 10:5.

The Redemptive Value of Suffering

1. Luke 13:12–13.
2. Luke 13:14.
3. Luke 13:15–16.
4. Mark 5:27–28.
5. Mark 5:29–30.
6. Mark 5:31–33.
7. Mark 5:34.
8. 2 Corinthians 12:7.
9. Ibid.
10. John 8:44.
11. The Catholic Company, "Saint Bernadette of Lourdes and Her Lessons on Suffering." Accessed July 10, 2017: https://www.catholiccompany.com/getfed/st-bernadette-lessons-suffering.
12. Catholic Herald, "Saint Bernadette Teaches Us How to Embrace Suffering." Accessed July 10, 2017: http://www.catholicherald.co.uk/commentandblogs/2015/02/11/st-bernadette-teaches-us-how-to-embrace-suffering.
13. John 10:10.
14. Job 2:7.
15. Matthew 8:16–17.
16. 2 Corinthians 12:7.
17. 2 Corinthians 12:9.
18. 2 Corinthians 12:7.

Dream Channeling with Fallen Angels

1. Daniel 1:16–17.
2. Daniel 2:2–3.
3. Daniel 2:4.
4. Daniel 2:5–6.
5. Daniel 2:7.
6. Daniel 2:8–9.
7. Daniel 2:10–11.
8. Daniel 2:15.
9. Daniel 2:16.
10. Daniel 2:17–19.
11. Acts 9:10–11.
12. Acts 10:9.

Receiving Demonic Impartations
1. Matthew 17:2 & 17:5–6.
2. Matthew 17:7.
3. Acts 3:4–8.
4. Acts 4:8.

Vows & Spiritually Binding Agreements
1. Judges 11:30–31.
2. Judges 11:34–37.
3. Judges 11:39.
4. Genesis 28:15–17.
5. Genesis 28:20–22.
6. Louis-Marie, Grignon de Montfort, *A Treatise on the True Devotion to the Blessed Virgin* (London: Burns and Lambert, 1863), p. 191.
7. Catechism of the Catholic Church: 827, Cf. *1 Jn* 1:8–10.
8. Louis-Marie, Grignon de Montfort, *A Treatise on the True Devotion to the Blessed Virgin* (London: Burns and Lambert, 1863), p. 191.
9. Luke 1:47–48.
10. Louis-Marie, Grignon de Montfort, *A Treatise on the True Devotion to the Blessed Virgin* (London: Burns and Lambert, 1863), p. 192.
11. Jeremiah 44:2–4.
12. Jeremiah 44:15–17.
13. Jeremiah 44:17–19.
14. Jeremiah 44:27.

The Sin of Idolatry Occurs in the Heart
1. 1 Corinthians 10:19–20.

Beware of Demonic Religious Spirits
1. 2 Corinthians 11:13–15.
2. Matthew 23:6–7.
3. Matthew 23:13–15 & 33.
4. Matthew 7:23.
5. Ibid.
6. Ibid.

Interaction with Fallen Angels of Light
1. Daniel 10:5–6.
2. Daniel 10:9–14.

Praying to Unknown Spiritual Entities

1. Matthew 15:22–23.
2. Matthew 15:24–27.
3. Matthew 15:28.
4. Catechism of the Catholic Church: 1280.
5. Exodus 20:5–6.
6. Exodus 20:5.
7. Catechism of the Catholic Church: 2663–2745.
8. Catechism of the Catholic Church: 823, *LG* 12, *Acts* 9:13, *1 Cor* 6:1, *1 Cor* 16:1.
9. Ephesians 1:1.
10. Catechism of the Catholic Church: 2114, Origen, *Contra Celsum* 2, 40: PG 11, 861.

The Importance of Emotional Healing

1. Matthew 18:1.
2. Matthew 18:3–4.
3. 2 Corinthians 2:11.

Renouncing Lodges & Secret Societies

1. *Initiation Ceremony into Freemasonry*. Accessed July 10, 2017: https://www.youtube.com/watch?v=wJrX5xuysx4.
2. John 8:12.
3. *The Deadly Deception: Freemasonry Exposed by One of its Top Leaders*. Accessed July 10, 2017: https://www.youtube.com/watch?v=8UpjPzdBaGo.
4. Congregation for the Doctrine of the Faith, "Irreconcilability Between Christian Faith and Freemasonry" (Vatican City, Rome: March 11, 1985), http://www.vatican.va/roman_curia/congregations/cfaith/documents/rc_con_cfaith_doc_19850223_declaration-masonic_articolo_en.html.

Denouncing Cults that Deny the Trinity

1. *The Occult: Mormons Are Satanic*. Accessed July 10, 2017: https://www.youtube.com/watch?v=b3lmWszMRTU.
2. *Mormon Secrets: What the Missionaries Don't Tell*. Accessed July 10, 2017: https://www.youtube.com/watch?v=-VKT4hrBTuk.
3. *The Secret World of Mormonism*. Accessed July 10, 2017:

https://www.youtube.com/watch?v=n3BqLZ8UoZk&list=PLlsdzL Dex56UephvA-ZI2idDZeN9Ad-rX.

4. *Behind the Veil: Never Before Seen Videos of Secret Mormon Temple Rituals.* Accessed July 10, 2017: https://www.youtube.com/ watch?v=6udew9axmdM.

5. Ibid.

6. *Secret Mormon Temple Handshakes with Hidden Camera.* Accessed July 10, 2017: https://www.youtube.com/ watch?v=x32JdymmF_Q.

7. The Mormon Curtain, "How Mormons Receive the Garments and How the Ceremony is Performed in the Temple." Accessed July 10, 2017: http://mormoncurtain.com/topic_garments_section1. html.

8. *What Jehovah's Witnesses Actually Believe.* Accessed July 10, 2017: https://www.youtube.com/watch?v=QzSwBsgHHXI.

9. Ibid.

10. Jehovah's Witnesses, "New World Translation of the Holy Scriptures." Accessed July 10, 2017: https://www.jw.org/en/ publications/bible/nwt/books/john/1.

11. Matthew 7:23.

12. Catechism of the Catholic Church: 266, Athanasian Creed; DS 75; ND 16.

13. Catechism of the Catholic Church: 260, Cf. *Jn* 17:21–23.

Developing a Deeper Relationship with God

1. Luke 11:14.

2. Luke 11:24–26.

3. Luke 11:24.

4. Luke 11:26.

5. Matthew 25:23.

The Catholic Warrior

The Catholic Warrior takes readers through spiritual boot camp and teaches them to draw on the power of Christ through the sacraments of the Church and the Word of God. It concludes with the Great Commission for those who are willing to accept the challenge and join the ranks.

Stories of men and women performing deeds of valor on the spiritual battlefield didn't end in Bible times or with the lives of saints from centuries past. Particularly in an era when priests are few and challenges are many, Christ needs laypeople who are willing to put on the full armor of God, push back enemy lines, and advance the kingdom of heaven here on earth.

Are you ready for an adventure of a lifetime? Rise to your feet, all you mighty warriors. The Spirit of God says, "Come!" You are hereby commissioned!

Available at your local bookstore or online at
www.CatholicWarriors.com

144 Pages — $8.99 U.S.

ABOUT THE AUTHOR

Robert Abel's purpose and passion in life is speaking God's truth unto today's generation. He lives in Denver, Colorado, where he leads a homeless ministry and helps others heal through counseling sessions and healing seminars.

If you would like Robert to speak at your parish, please contact him at: **www.CatholicDeliverance.com**

If you would like to participate in our healing and deliverance ministry, please consider distributing copies of the *Catholic Deliverance Manual* to your friends and family members. To purchase additional copies, please use the following information:

Number of Copies	Ministry Price
3	$35
6	$55
9	$75

These prices include tax and free shipping within the United States. For shipments to other countries, please contact us. Thank you for your generous support.

Mail your payment to:

Valentine Publishing House
Catholic Deliverance Manual
P.O. Box 27422
Denver, Colorado 80227